Builders & Decorators

Medieval Craftsmen in Wales

Nicola Coldstream

Introduction

In the twelfth-century priory church at Penmon on Anglesey there is a stone fragment carved with the image of a bearded man. The figure, probably of the same date as the church, is weathered and battered, but clutched in his right hand remains a mason's axe. After the passage of more than eight centuries, its full significance eludes us. It is appealing to imagine that the sculptor fashioned it to represent himself or one of his fellows, but it is not a portrait in any modern sense and may never have been anything more than a simple image of a mason. Nevertheless, the figure serves to remind us that an army of largely unrecorded and frequently forgotten craftsmen worked to raise and decorate the buildings of medieval Wales. It is their labours and the legacy of their skills — many of which are still in use today — that this book sets out to celebrate.

Little monumental building in stone survives from the period before the arrival of the Normans in Wales, not long after 1066, and no standing timber structures survive from such an early date. We therefore know very little about building conditions or craftsmen before the twelfth century. Some sculptors signed their work: Sciloc carved his name on an eleventh-century memorial cross at Merthyr Mawr, near Bridgend (Glamorgan), and in the same century Menhir signed the stone font in the church of St Ishow at Partrishow in Breconshire. But these are exceptional cases. With the Normans came greater building activity and more sophisticated constructional methods. And, as the importance of written documents increased over the centuries, more evidence of the craftsmen — masons, sculptors, carpenters, painters, tilers and glaziers — has survived. Yet documentary records of building in medieval Wales remain scarce and sporadic, and only rarely name individual craftsmen: Master James of St George (d. 1308/9) at the late thirteenth-century royal castles in north Wales and Master Thomas de la Bataile at Caerphilly Castle (Glamorgan) in 1326 are exceptions, not the rule. The overwhelming majority of craftsmen remain unknown, and the only record of their skills survives in great monumental edifices — castles, cathedrals and monasteries — and in more humble buildings — houses, cottages and parish churches.

These buildings also reveal much about the relationship of Wales with its neighbours in Ireland and England and its contacts with more distant parts of the medieval world. The men who erected them often travelled far to ply their craft and brought with them artistic styles and construction techniques that can be traced in the fabric and decoration of the structures.

Despite the often turbulent history of Wales, succeeding generations of princes and churchmen, and indeed the population at large, built and rebuilt their castles, churches and homes throughout the Middle Ages. Far from being daunted by strife, the conditions stimulated them to strengthen their castles and replace burned monasteries. Their desire for salvation and an eternity in Paradise made them anxious to adorn their churches. The

The twelfth-century carving of a mason in the priory church at Penmon on Anglesey — an enigmatic reminder of the multitude of unidentified craftsmen who laboured to construct the buildings of medieval Wales (ffotograff).

Opposite: Although the abbey church at Tintern (Monmouthshire) stands roofless and empty, these majestic piers and arches bear witness to the skill and artistry of the medieval craftsmen who built and decorated the church in the late thirteenth and early fourteenth centuries.

This detail from a manuscript illustration of about 1250 depicts a busy contemporary building site. Similar scenes would have been familiar in Wales throughout the Middle Ages as strife, devotion and changing architectural fashions stimulated the building and rebuilding of castles, churches and homes (©Photo SCALA, Florence 2004 — The Pierpont Morgan Library, New York, Ms. M. 638, f. 3).

devotional images presented in carvings, wall paintings and stained glass also provided religious instruction for the illiterate. As a result, many buildings boast art and architecture from several periods and embody the contributions of generations of craftsmen.

This book explores how craftsmen set about their tasks of building and decorating during the period between about 1100 and 1536, when King Henry VIII forced the closure of the monasteries and a new chapter in building history began. Although such portable objects as illuminated manuscripts, embroidered hangings and works in precious metals were important to the occupants, here we are concerned with the physical structure and decoration of buildings. By examining what influenced the design of buildings as well as the craftsmen's techniques, we can better appreciate the great legacy of medieval builders and decorators in Wales.

Networks of Influence

For all its mountain barriers and intricate coastline, medieval Wales was not sealed off from the rest of the world. The river Severn and the Bristol Channel in the south and the river Dee in the north were conduits for international trade, materials and people. Already, before the advent of the Normans there was much artistic interchange with the areas bordering Wales to the east, the Cheshire plain, and south-west England. There had also been regular, fruitful contacts with early Christian Ireland and, later, some influence came from Vikings who had settled on the coasts of Britain and Ireland and the Isle of Man.

Norman influence came inevitably in the wake of 1066. The Normans' arrival was to have the same impact on Wales as it did on England. Countless earth-and-timber castles were thrown up to consolidate their advance, but they also built massive, beautifully finished stone towers, or donjons — as at Chepstow in Monmouthshire — protecting a nearby priory church. St Mary's Church in Chepstow, with its thick walls, solid piers and decorated doorways influenced by contemporary architecture in Normandy, contrasts strongly with local traditions. But the Welsh were also in close touch with France. Artistic influences came not only with the craftsmen, but also from patrons — individual lords and bishops and the religious orders that had their origins in France.

Patronage is as much about self-image as about the need for a roof over your head. Self-image can take two forms: propaganda and identity. The propagandist element is clear in the massive Norman great tower at Chepstow and the monumental castles of Edward I (1272–1307) in north Wales; it is also evident in the equally assertive castles of the Welsh princes, such as Cricieth built by the Gwynedd prince, Llywelyn ab Iorwerth 'the Great' (d. 1240). Nor did such patrons rely only on massive towers

Below left: The great tower of Chepstow Castle (Monmouthshire) is one of the earliest and most imposing of the massive stone towers, or donjons, erected by the Normans as they pushed into Wales after 1066.

Below: The richly ornamented, late eleventh-century western doorway of the former priory church of St Mary at Chepstow reflects the influence of contemporary architecture in Normandy rather than local traditions.

Above: This fine stone head found amidst the ruins of Deganwy Castle (Caernarfonshire) may represent its builder, Llywelyn ab Iorwerth, 'the Great', the powerful prince of Gwynedd who dominated native Wales in the thirteenth century until his death in 1240. Carving of this quality proclaimed a patron's wealth and refinement (National Museum of Wales).

Right: When Llywelyn ab Iorwerth built his new castle at Cricieth (Caernarfonshire), probably between 1230 and 1240, he provided it with a massive twin-towered gatehouse of an advanced design. Even before it was later raised in height, the gatehouse was an imposing structure and it unmistakably asserted Llywelyn's power as the pre-eminent native ruler in Wales.

and walls to assert their power and sophistication: the delicate carved decoration at Llywelyn's castles at Deganwy (Caernarfonshire) and Castell y Bere (Merioneth) shows that money paid to talented sculptors was money well spent.

Self-image as identity appears in religious houses, especially the Cistercian abbeys, whose ties to France survived until the Reformation in the mid-sixteenth century. Welsh monasteries reflected influential French models in their general plans, as well as their architectural details. The Cistercian abbey of Strata Florida in Ceredigion was also important to Welsh identity: not only was it the burial place of the Deheubarth dynasty of princes, who ruled south-west Wales, but it was also a major centre for cultural and political activity.

Yet, while Strata Florida proclaims the political power of its patron, Rhys ap Gruffudd, the Lord Rhys (d. 1197), it also helps to demonstrate the limits of his architectural influence. Rhys was also the patron of Talley, an abbey in Carmarthenshire belonging to the Premonstratensian order, which originated in France and had much in common with the Cistercians. Yet, although Rhys endowed both abbeys and contributed handsomely to the building of their churches, he had very little say in their design or appearance. Instead, the abbeys' buildings reflected the ideals of austerity and the practicalities of observance that then prevailed in the two orders. The buildings of Strata Florida, for instance, contained provision for the lay brothers who were a significant feature of the early centuries of the Cistercian movement. In contrast, such

provision is lacking at Talley because lay brothers — never so important among the Premonstratensians — played little or no role in the community.

Some designs seem to have taken root in Wales as part of a general movement of craftsmen from the west of England to Ireland. Details of the vault and architectural sculpture at the twelfth-century priory church of Ewenny in the Vale of Glamorgan are so similar to those at Cormac's Chapel at Cashel in Ireland's county Tipperary that we must presume they had a common source, possibly Gloucester.

A few resident builders and carpenters have left traces in the record, but many more craftsmen were itinerant and travelled beyond Wales or came from outside it, often from far afield. Master Ralph Gogun of London, for instance, is recorded at Chepstow in the 1280s and is known to have worked at nearby Tintern Abbey in Monmouthshire, as well as at Chipping Sodbury, just across the river Severn in England. The carpenters, diggers and masons impressed to build Edward I's castles in Snowdonia after the second Welsh war of 1282–83 numbered some 1,650 and came from almost every county in England. However, James of St George, the master of works in charge of the entire project, was brought from the distant county of Savoy in the southern Alps.

This influx of craftsmen continued in the early fourteenth century. Thomas de la Bataile, the master mason at Caerphilly Castle, had worked in Kent. His colleague at Caerphilly, William Hurley (d. 1354), had already served the king as a master carpenter at Westminster; he would go on to distinguish himself in further work for the Crown and at Ely Cathedral in East Anglia.

Above: The Lord Rhys was a generous benefactor to Strata Florida Abbey (Ceredigion), but he would have had little say in the design of its buildings (Skyscan Balloon Photography, for Cadw).

The priory church at Ewenny (Glamorgan), which shows the influence of designs from the west of England in the details of its vault and architectural sculpture.

Master James of St George

The best-known medieval mason in Wales is Master James of St George (d. 1308/9). He was the master mason of Edward I's castles from 1278 until about 1300. He organized the supply of men and materials and the building work at many of the castles raised during and after the Welsh wars, most notably at Rhuddlan (Flintshire), Harlech (Merioneth), Conwy and Caernarfon (Caernarfonshire) and Beaumaris (Anglesey), with work often going on simultaneously at several sites.

Master James was neither Welsh nor English. Edward I summoned him from the county of Savoy, now in parts of modern France, Switzerland and Italy. There he had worked for Edward's great-uncle, Count Philip of Savoy (d. 1285), on a series of castles and projects for new towns around the lakes of Geneva and Neuchâtel, including Chillon and Yverdon. At St Georges d'Espéranche, which may have been his birthplace, James took part in the construction of a residence for Philip.

Master James brought over several masons from Savoy. These men used a number of construction methods and design details — for example, the corbelled latrine outlet and window tracery at Harlech — that are found in Savoy, but were previously unknown in buildings in Wales.

Master James worked with senior assistants, Richard the Engineer and Walter of Hereford, who were master masons themselves and probably directed everyday operations on site. James's task as overseer and administrator of the project was so time-consuming that he did not design the castles himself, except possibly Beaumaris. Edward valued him for his outstanding abilities as an organizer who was able to run a vast and expensive building campaign, and negotiate with an exceptionally demanding patron.

This early fourteenth-century manuscript illustration depicts a king in discussion with his master mason. King Edward I (1272–1307) held similar conferences with Master James of St George (d. 1308/9) and other master masons during the construction of the royal castles in north Wales (© British Library Board, Cotton Nero D. 1, f. 23v).

Above: A window at Harlech Castle in Merioneth (reconstructed left) shows similarities to one in the Savoyard castle of Saillon (right), now in Switzerland.

Right: Although he was primarily occupied with the supervision of Edward I's castle-building programme in Wales, Master James may have designed the castle at Beaumaris on Anglesey.

The doorway to the porch of the bishop's hall at St Davids Bishop's Palace in Pembrokeshire has an unusual arch head shaped from four sides of an octagon. It was erected in the latter stages of the extensive remodelling of the palace by Bishop Henry de Gower (1328–47) in the 1330s and 1340s.

The doorway to the porch of the great hall in Berkeley Castle, Gloucestershire, also exhibits an arch head derived from four sides of an octagon. The Berkeley Castle arch was probably completed about 1343–45, and its resemblance to the one at St Davids makes it likely that they were both executed by the same master mason (David Price/BCCT).

Throughout the fourteenth century, the Bristol Channel was a conduit of artistic traffic between the flourishing port of Bristol and various places in south Wales, including Tintern Abbey and the bishop's palace at St Davids (Pembrokeshire). At St Davids, the style of sculpture and the use of an arch head shaped from four sides of an octagon shows clear similarities with work carried out for the Berkeley family of Berkeley Castle in Gloucestershire; it is likely that the same master mason was responsible for both. At Tintern, the great stone pulpitum screen that once divided the nave from the choir in the abbey church was constructed about 1325–30 (p. 37). The masons were working to designs that may anticipate better-known examples in Bristol, Wells and other cathedrals and churches of south-west England, produced under the direction of the master mason, Thomas of Witney (d. 1342), with the collaboration of fellow master, William Joy.

The counties bordering Wales were also significant sources of stained glass and floor tiles right to the end of the Middle Ages. Thomas Stanley (d. 1504), first earl of Derby, gave stained glass to All Saints' Church, Gresford (Denbighshire) around 1500 (see pp. 57–58). The Stanley family were associated with several buildings in the northern Marches at about that time, including the church of St Mary at Mold (Flintshire) around 1490, and St Winifred's Well at Holywell (Flintshire), where Stanley emblems appear in the vault of the well chapel (p. 36).

The Perpendicular-style tower of St Giles's Church, a prominent landmark in the north Wales border town of Wrexham (Denbighshire), has a fussy profile with crowded pinnacles, a design based on the central tower of Gloucester Cathedral, which was built in the 1450s and influenced a number of other building schemes. Either the master mason of Wrexham had worked at Gloucester or he was sent to copy the design. It is one of the intriguing puzzles of the networks of artistic influence in this period that the possibilities are numerous, but the answers rarely clear or simple.

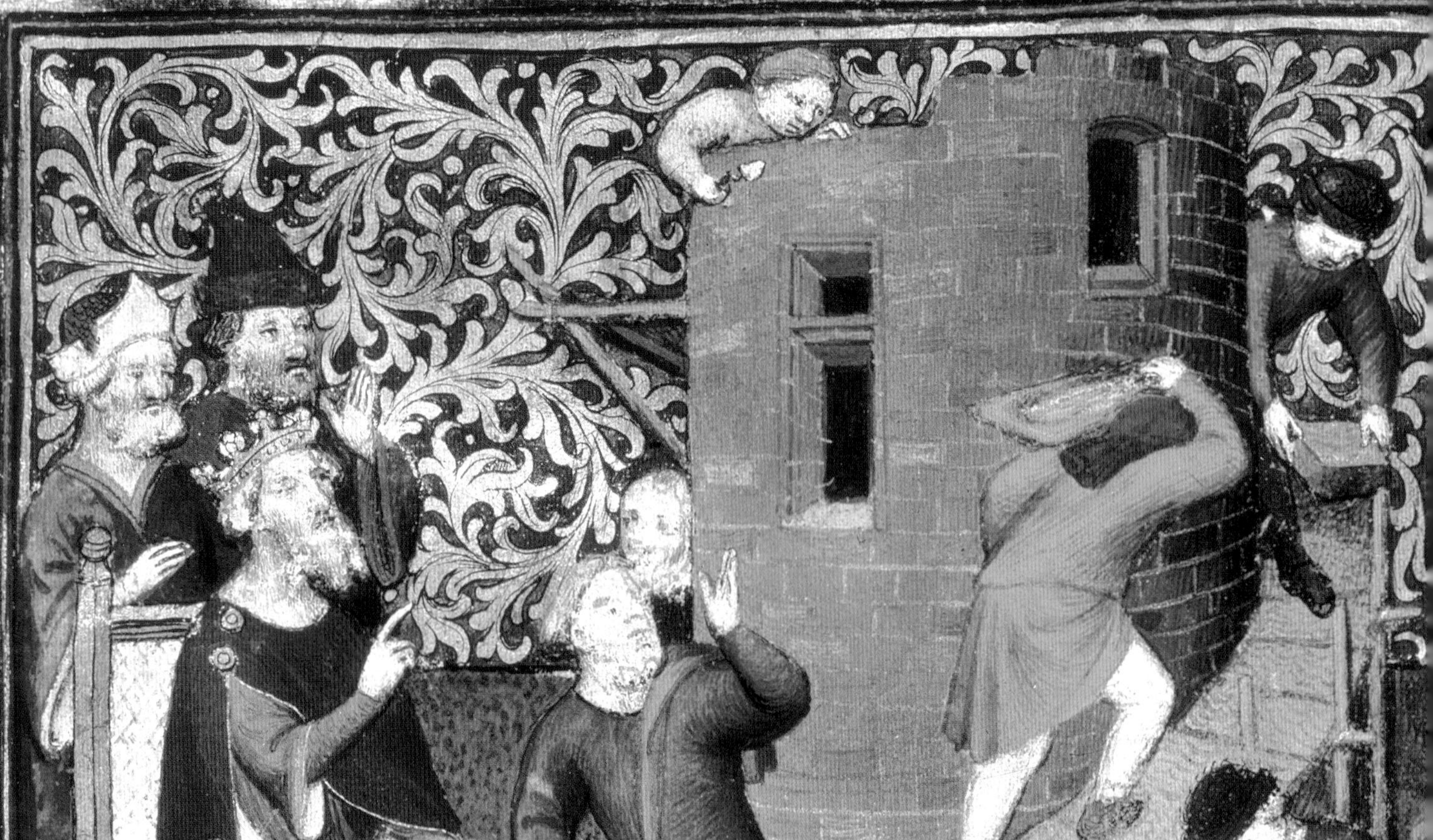

The Craftsmen

Within, in the middle of the enclosure, the master-builders constructed a tower with great skill. There could not be a more beautiful one, for it was large and broad and tall. The walls should not give way to any machinery for throwing missiles, for the mortar was made of quicklime soaked in strong vinegar. The stone from which they made the foundation was the native rock, as hard as diamond. The tower was completely round; in all the world was none so rich or better arranged within.

Guillaume de Lorris and Jean de Meun, *The Romance of the Rose*, trans. C. Dahlberg.
© 1971 Princeton University Press, 1999 renewed PUP Reprinted by permission of Princeton University Press.

This passage from the great medieval allegorical poem, *The Romance of the Rose* — written by Guillaume de Lorris between 1225 and 1230 — could easily be a description of the massive early thirteenth-century round tower of Pembroke Castle (Pembrokeshire). While the stronghold in the poem is a metaphorical castle of love, the poet has gone to considerable trouble to give us some information about the masons and their building methods. As they listened, his audience would have been able to envisage the construction of the tower from their own experience. So universal was the culture within which the poem was written, that an aristocratic audience in Wales would have responded in the same way as a contemporary audience elsewhere in Europe.

Nowadays, the technical skill required to design and build a complicated medieval structure without powered machines or computers is awe inspiring. The two most important people on the building site were the master mason and the master carpenter. Their expertise was much sought after; they enjoyed equal status and

A manuscript illustration showing how an artist of about 1490–1500 imagined the tower described in The Romance of the Rose *after completion (© British Library Board, Harley Ms. 4425, f. 39).*

The great round tower at Pembroke Castle (Pembrokeshire), not unlike that described in The Romance of the Rose, *still soars above the other buildings of the castle. It was built by William Marshal (d. 1219), earl of Pembroke, shortly after 1204.*

Opposite: In this early fifteenth-century manuscript illustration, craftsmen toil to build a round tower like the one described in The Romance of the Rose. *To the right, a mason dresses stone, while a labourer carries a tray of mortar up a spiral (helicoidal) scaffolding ramp to the men laying the squared blocks (© British Library Board, Royal Ms. 15 D. III, f. 15v).*

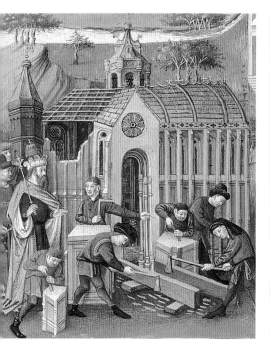

Above: The cooperation between masons and carpenters required in the construction of a stone building is suggested in this mid-fifteenth-century manuscript illustration (Bibliothèque Nationale de France, Ms. Latin 4915, f. 46v).

Above right: A reconstruction of the great hall at Caerphilly Castle (Glamorgan) upon which the master carpenter, William Hurley (d. 1354), worked with the master mason, Thomas de la Bataile, in 1326. Little evidence survives for the structure of William Hurley's splendid open timber roof, so the details shown here are conjectural (Illustration by Terry Ball, 1989; with modifications, 1997).

Right: William Hurley's manuscript receipt for the payment for his work at Caerphilly (The National Archives/Public Record Office, E101/127/21, no. 6).

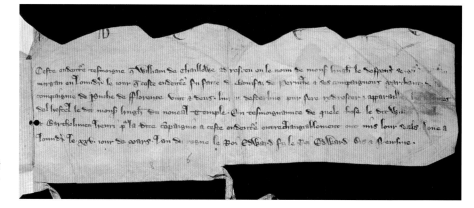

could command high fees. On stone buildings they worked closely together, as at Caerphilly in 1326 when the master carpenter, William Hurley, worked alongside the master mason, Thomas de la Bataile, almost certainly extending the great hall and putting in place a splendid open timber roof. Ensuring that the heavy wooden roof was compatible with the stone structure below was often their most important joint task: the flexibility of timber allows it to move in response to wind, humidity and changes in temperature, and the rigid stonework beneath had to be able to withstand the forces that the roof generated.

The cellar of the late thirteenth-century hall block at Chepstow Castle shows how far masons and carpenters sometimes had to cooperate. The cellar was built across a natural fissure in the cliff above the river Wye, and the carpenters had to bridge the gap with a platform of wooden beams. This platform supported the wooden centering or formwork (p. 31) over which the masons constructed a stone vault to support the cellar. To achieve this extraordinary piece of engineering, the carpenters and masons had to work in perilous conditions high above the strongly flowing river. Without complete trust between them, it would have been impossible.

Very little of the craftsmen's activity is documented. Most of the evidence is indirect. It comes from building accounts — records of wages and materials; contracts; building regulations; wills; and sometimes the criminal court. What we do not have, until the very late fifteenth century, is any sort of treatise on building or written theory of architecture. Even then, such works are misleading in several ways and none is known to have been written in Wales. Since we know comparatively few craftsmen by name we cannot make the critical examination of their careers that is possible for more recent architects, such as John Nash (1752–1835) in the Regency period or William Burges (1827–81) in the Victorian era.

Yet we can find out a surprising amount from such records as there are, and, of course, from the buildings themselves. That so many are in ruins is not necessarily a disadvantage. In some ways a building is like the human body: we may admire the exterior, but if we want to know how it is constructed we need to look beneath the surface. The best areas for observing and understanding building techniques are the damaged parts — arches and vaults that are half fallen, exposed joints or decayed walls. Exposed masonry in the gatehouse of Raglan Castle in Monmouthshire, for instance, shows evidence of a vault that no longer exists.

In the rest of this book we shall look at many aspects of medieval building, from the craftsmen themselves and how they organized their businesses to the structures, techniques and decoration. The craftsmen who added the finishing touches were as essential as the masons and carpenters, and all left their mark on buildings in Wales.

Modern wooden centering in use to support an arch under construction (National Museum of Wales).

Below left: The creation of the cellar beneath the late thirteenth-century hall block at Chepstow Castle required the closest cooperation between carpenters and masons. Working high above the river Wye, the carpenters had to bridge a fissure in the rock before the centering for the cellar's supporting vault could be constructed.

Below: Evidence of a now-vanished vault in the masonry of the gatehouse at Raglan Castle (Monmouthshire).

Comit on edifia la tour de babiloine. et le languege fust mue en .lxxij. languegez. et les anges la despererunt.

The Masons

The man in overall charge of the building site was the master mason. He was a remarkable individual: designer, engineer and contractor all in one. Medieval builders did not distinguish between the roles of what would nowadays be the work of three different professionals.

Although there is early evidence of monks acting as architects, particularly on Cistercian sites, by the thirteenth century masons and other craftsmen were almost invariably laymen. The master mason was essentially a builder, who received his training at the quarry and on the building site. The best or most ambitious masons also learned design skills, rising through the ranks of ordinary masons — journeymen — to become masters and take charge of building projects. Yet they still continued to take an active part in building and this experience was vital to their understanding of how to design a safe structure. The master was always present, except on large-scale projects, such as Edward I's programme of castle building in north Wales, or in the later Middle Ages when a successful master had built up a large practice; in these circumstances his place was taken by an under-master. Andrew Cole, for instance, seems to have acted as foreman to the master mason, Richard More, at Newport Castle (Monmouthshire) in the mid-fifteenth century.

Opposite: Many of the tools and practices of late medieval masons are shown in this manuscript illustration. This scene from the early fifteenth-century Bedford Hours *shows the building of the Tower of Babel (© British Library Board, Additional Ms. 18850, f. 554v).*

In the wake of his 1282–83 campaign, King Edward I mobilized massive labour forces to undertake the simultaneous construction of brand new strongholds at Caernarfon, seen here, and Conwy (Caernarfonshire) and Harlech (Merioneth).

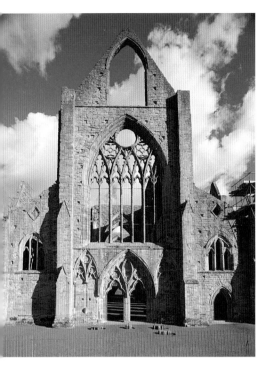

Monmouthshire's lower Wye valley witnessed considerable building activity in the closing decades of the thirteenth century. The monks of Tintern Abbey, latterly enjoying the patronage of Roger Bigod, fifth earl of Norfolk (d. 1306), consecrated their new abbey church (above) in 1301, more than thirty years after its construction had begun in 1269. At Earl Roger's nearby castle at Chepstow, extensive works included the construction of the elaborate new domestic range that stands perched on the cliff edge above the Wye (above right). Ralph Gogun (d. 1293), the master mason responsible for much of the work at Chepstow, also worked at Tintern, and similarities in architectural details suggest the movement of a group of masons between the sites.

The master mason often contracted to provide a team of journeymen masons himself. Yet even when he did so, there is only occasional evidence that they formed a coherent group, moving as a team from site to site. Detailed similarities between the works at Tintern Abbey and Chepstow Castle, carried out for Roger Bigod, fifth earl of Norfolk (d. 1306) in the late thirteenth century, suggest that the same group of masons moved between the two buildings, but this is a rare example. The idea that all medieval masons were members of permanent associations, or lodges, is misleading. It derives from some atypical evidence from late medieval Germany, which was crystallized into 'fact' by the later Brotherhood of Freemasons.

The masons' lodge was not an institution, but a temporary building that acted as a workshop for the more delicate carving, as a safe store for the masons' tools, and as a sheltered retreat for rest and food. Because it was usually built of timber, its construction was the carpenters' first task at the beginning of a new building project. Normally, when work came to an end, the lodge was dismantled and the masons went their separate ways.

As accounting systems become more detailed in the later Middle Ages we can see that the builders were differentiated by the tasks they performed. The lowliest workers on the site were labourers, who were not masons at all. Labourers dug ditches and foundation trenches, and carried away the unwanted earth. There were always more labourers than skilled masons: during a typical week at Caernarfon Castle in 1295, there were fewer than one hundred masons, but more than two hundred labourers. For this great enterprise some labourers were brought from England, but at other sites the labourers were usually Welsh. At Newport Castle in the fifteenth century there were five Welsh labourers and one, Philip Irish, presumably from Ireland.

The masons themselves were categorized as rough masons and freemasons. These terms have nothing to do with liberty. Rough masons were unskilled, whereas freemasons were skilled men who could cut, or dress, freestone (stone that could be worked with or against the grain without developing a fault) to create even, squared blocks — ashlars — or more complex moulded shapes. Quarrymen were differentiated from masons, and the 1402 accounts for work at Kidwelly Castle (Carmarthenshire) distinguish between masons, stonebreakers and stone carriers. Such names as Dafydd ab Ithel and Ieuan Owyn show that most of the eight masons working there through April were Welsh.

In addition to a higher rate of pay than his assistants, a master mason enjoyed several benefits in the way of food, drink and robes; and the patron often lent or rented him a house for the duration of the building programme. Frequently, the master mason submitted a claim for a lump sum for his workers' wages, as at Chepstow, where Master Ralph Gogun was paid £6 11s. for three summer months. This amount was to cover the wages of masons, quarrymen and others who were working on the new kitchen. Master Ralph also sent in a claim for the carpenters' wages and on one occasion, when he was away at Chipping Sodbury, the wages claim was handled by an assistant, John de Wolauston. Some building accounts, however, specify the pay of individuals: the men working at Kidwelly in 1402 were individually listed and each paid 4d. per day. Their leader, John Herd, at the top of the list, was paid 3s. 4d. per week.

In this fifteenth-century manuscript illustration, freemasons cut elaborate moulded blocks under the shelter of a timber masons' lodge. The lodge was not only a workshop; it also provided masons with a place where they could rest, eat and safely store their tools. This detailed scene also depicts many other operations involved in the erection of a stone building. Labourers mix mortar (centre) and move carved stones, while masons lay the fine ashlar walls of a new church. Straw is also shown placed on top of an unfinished wall to protect the masonry from the weather (Bibliothèque Royale de Belgique, Ms. 6, f. 554v).

Designing the Building

What set the master mason apart from his journeyman assistants was his ability to draw up designs. His first task was to agree the building design with the patron. Some wording to this effect was usually included in the formal contract, together with the expected rate of building. Since a more elaborate design would cost more money, the patron was actively involved from the start. The patron dictated the main outlines and the number of storeys and chapels or rooms. Some took more interest in the designs than others. Just as nowadays, there were always people who had no idea what they wanted, while others made informed choices, specifying the layout of a church or the plan of a castle, and closely followed the building's progress. Edward I even issued instructions to individual masons working at the castles of Conwy and Aberystwyth (Ceredigion). But no patron possessed the practical knowledge of design techniques that enabled masons to convert plans and patterns into stone. This depended on the master mason.

The master mason had to be able to think in three dimensions, both on a large and a small scale. He made detailed designs for everything from the ground plan and elevations to the piers, arches and window tracery, devising the profiles of their mouldings. His drawing instruments were the compasses, the straightedge and the L-shaped square, used to produce right angles. General designs, particularly if they were to be shown to the patron, could be made on parchment and detailed with colour. On the other hand, working drawings for elements of a building, such as window tracery patterns or profiles of mouldings for piers or arches, were made at full size on boards or a plaster surface prepared for the purpose. Sometimes they were incised on walls or the floor — medieval tracing floors still exist at the English cathedrals of Wells and York.

A royal patron inspects a building site in the company of his master mason in this mid-thirteenth-century illustration by the chronicler, Matthew Paris. While some patrons did little more than approve a building's main features, others took an active interest in the finer points of the design and closely followed the progress of construction (Trinity College Library, Ms. 177, f. 59v — The Board of Trinity College, Dublin).

A drawing of the late medieval tracing floor at York Minster. Some of the designs can be matched to existing windows in the church (By kind permission of the Dean and Chapter of York: © Dean and Chapter of York).

Opposite: During the building of Conwy Castle, King Edward I issued instructions to individual masons. Edward — an experienced soldier who had campaigned in Britain and Europe and on crusade in the Holy Land — undoubtedly acted as a discerning patron at every stage in the construction of the royal castles built in Wales after the wars of 1276–77 and 1282–83.

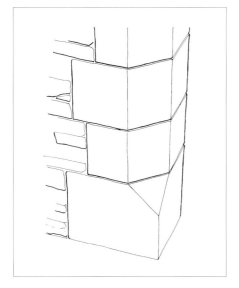

Above: A diagonal chamfer — the simplest of mouldings — was created by cutting the corner off a squared block at an angle of 45 degrees.

Above right: A modern mason uses a template to mark out a block in preparation for cutting.

Right: The massive cylindrical nave piers in the church of St Cadfan in Tywyn (Merioneth) probably date from the 1140s. The piers in Welsh Romanesque churches of the late eleventh and early twelfth centuries are generally cylindrical or rectangular and unadorned with mouldings (ffotograff).

Below: A moulding profile of one of the thirteenth-century piers in the east end of the abbey church at Tintern. The master mason created an elaborate design with shafts embellished with keels and fillets.

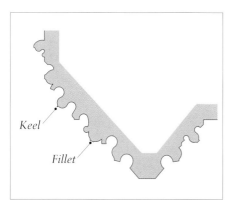

Keel

Fillet

The designed profiles were the basis of templates for all the carved stones. The masons used them to mark stone blocks with the lines and points that would guide their cutting. Templates were made of wood or metal, unless they were to be taken to the quarry, when some light material, such as canvas, was used.

The mouldings for piers and arches were cut from blocks that were basically cubic or cylindrical. The simplest kind of moulding — the diagonal chamfer — is produced by slicing off the corner of a square block at an angle of 45 degrees. The piers in the surviving Romanesque churches of late eleventh- and early twelfth-century Wales rarely exhibited even such a basic moulding and were generally cylindrical, like those at the church of St Cadfan in Tywyn (Merioneth), or rectangular. As the Middle Ages progressed, however, mouldings became more varied and elaborate. The fourteenth-century piers at the church of St Mary in Haverfordwest

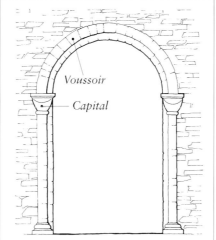

Far left: One of the fourteenth-century piers in the church of St Mary, Haverfordwest (Pembrokeshire). Purbeck Marble — a dark limestone from Dorset — has been incorporated into the design as separate, detached, shafts.

Above: The Romanesque doorway into the nave of St Woolos Cathedral in Newport (Monmouthshire). The individual blocks, or voussoirs, of the arch were carved before they were set in position, so the master mason had to set out their curvature as well as the details of the bold surface decoration.

Left: A simplified drawing of a Romanesque arch.

(Pembrokeshire) are made up of clusters of shafts or of stones cut to resemble separate shafts: here each shaft is embellished with either a raised fillet or a slightly pointed keel. The master mason devised complicated mouldings by indicating where hollows were to be gouged out of a block, creating projections and recesses.

Each piece of stone had to be shaped precisely to fit its place, and it was the master mason's responsibility to get the measurements and curvatures right. An arch, for example, is composed of individual wedge-shaped stones — voussoirs — which form the curve of the arch. The master had to design the curvature of the back and the sides of each individual stone, as well as the pattern or mouldings for the front surface. These could be elaborate, as on the Romanesque west doorway into the nave of St Woolos Cathedral, Newport (Monmouthshire), which is boldly ornamented with geometric patterns.

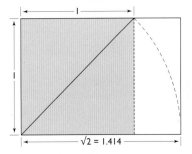

A rectangle with sides in the ratio of 1:√2 was often used by medieval craftsmen. It could be defined by rotating the diagonal of a square to the baseline. Although this could be easily done with simple instruments, medieval masons often relied upon approximations in sequences of √2 proportions such as 12:17:24:34.

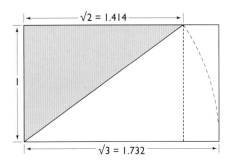

Another common ratio used in medieval buildings was 1:√3. This could be derived from the hypotenuse of a right angle triangle with sides in the ratio of 1:√2.

Systems of Proportion

Methods of designing medieval buildings were based on geometric figures — the triangle, the circle and the square — a practice now known as constructive geometry. Constructive geometry is entirely pragmatic. It is not based on theory, and it was taught by example as a series of practical steps. The masons' knowledge of constructive geometry may be the 'secrets' that are referred to in some late medieval craft regulations: secrets that were not to be revealed to outsiders or even to newcomers at the site. Yet constructive geometry is not at all difficult. Its operation is simple and flexible, exactly what was needed to produce such a complex structure as a vaulted building.

These geometric figures could be employed in a simple, additive fashion. For example, the plan of the nave, crossing and eastern arm of the thirteenth-century abbey church at Margam (Glamorgan) was defined by four squares with sides equal to the width of the existing twelfth-century church.

Masons also used triangles and squares to generate proportional ratios that could link one feature of the building with another. A common ratio is one to the square root of two (1:√2), which is easy to derive from a square. The diagonal of a square is the length of one side multiplied by √2; simply rotate the diagonal down to the base line to create a rectangle. Another common ratio, 1:√3, is derived from a triangle.

These ratios are very handy for making designs without the elaborate instruments and computers available to modern architects. Masons could generate all the proportions they needed from the basic square. On the largest scale, the ground plan of a church might comprise a √2 rectangle for the nave, with the transept and choir based on a triangle in proportion. The window shapes may be derived from the same basic measure, which could be reduced to produce such details as moulding profiles. No mathematics was involved. Apart from deciding the number of bays and so on, the only numerical calculations the masons used were the number systems developed to represent the geometric proportions so that the geometric figures did not have to be drawn out each time: for example, a sequence of √2 proportions might run 12:17:24:34. This is particularly useful, since the ratio between rectangles defined by successive pairs of these numbers, 12:17, 17:24 and so forth, is always 1:2. Thus, a sheet of A4 paper, which is a √2 rectangle, is twice the size of an A5 sheet.

The master mason who designed the thirteenth-century church at Margam Abbey (Glamorgan) used four squares in additive fashion as the basis for the plan of the nave, crossing and eastern arm.

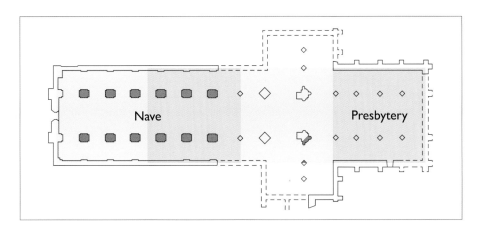

Preparations for Building

There is no structure more complicated than a medieval vaulted building. That such buildings were constructed at a time when no exact engineering calculations could be made, yet remain standing after hundreds of years, is testimony to the skill of the builders and the stability of the building material. The priory church at Ewenny still boasts its twelfth-century barrel and rib vaults, and even at Cymer, a humble Cistercian abbey in Merioneth, the arches of one of the nave arcades still stand.

Building was a seasonal activity. Like law terms and accounting periods, medieval building was conducted by the saints' calendar and it ran from the Feast of the Purification of the Virgin on 2 February until All Saints' Day on 1 November. Active building came to a halt during the winter months because the cold and damp inhibited the setting of the lime mortar used to bond the masonry; before it sets, mortar is vulnerable to freezing, which renders it useless. Nevertheless, a few masons were kept on to perform indoor tasks, such as making designs or carving small details at the bankers — or workbenches — in the lodge.

Before construction could begin the ground had to be prepared. The masons tested it for stability. If the chosen site was uneven they had to level it, sometimes cutting away a quantity of solid rock. This could be used for the building itself. The castles of Dolforwyn (Montgomeryshire) and Dinas Brân (Denbighshire) are built partly of the rock on which they stand.

The master mason's next important task was to visit the quarry to examine the stone beds and select the stone. The greater patrons often owned quarries, which could be a source for the building stone. By the late Middle Ages, some masons leased quarries as a business sideline, selling stone and supplying it for buildings on which they were working.

There was an active trade in stone, which could be transported over great distances. A significant source of freestone for buildings in south Wales was the Dundry Quarry,

The survival of one of the nave arcades at Cymer Abbey (Merioneth), a small Cistercian house at the foot of Cadair Idris, testifies to the skill of the masons who built it and the stability of their materials.

Newport Castle (Monmouthshire), where four cartloads of freestone from the Dundry Quarry, near Bristol, were delivered by water in 1435. The stone, which had been sawn into pieces before its shipment from Bristol, was dressed for its final use by masons in Newport.

The quarry at Grinshill in Shropshire was an important source of freestone for buildings in mid-Wales. This capital from Cwmhir Abbey (Radnorshire) was fashioned from Grinshill Sandstone. It is now in the church of St Idloes in Llanidloes (Montgomeryshire).

near Bristol. Limestone from Dundry was used in the twelfth century at Llandaff Cathedral (Glamorgan) and later in the work of William Marshal (d. 1219), lord of Chepstow and later earl of Pembroke, at his Monmouthshire castles of Chepstow, Usk and Caerleon. Records show that in 1435, the mason, Richard More, bought four cartloads of Dundry Stone for Newport Castle. It was carted to Bristol and sawn to pieces, ready for transport by water to Newport. There it was dressed — carved into building blocks — by three masons and four Welsh labourers.

Transport over land was very expensive, so waterways were used whenever possible. In 1317, a fully equipped 20-ton boat, the *St Mary* of Caernarfon, was bought for the works at that castle and for fetching supplies from Ireland and elsewhere. For all of Edward I's castles in north Wales, some building materials were brought in from distant sources. Iron and steel, for example, came from Newcastle-under-Lyme in Staffordshire, and like other materials, such as lead, coal and glass, they were collected at Chester and shipped down the river Dee.

The good-quality stone was kept for work above ground. For the foundations, mortared rubble was often brought from demolished structures. The master mason set out the ground plan with cords, pegs and lime, and the foundation trenches were then dug. The foundations were probably laid all around the building as soon as possible, since empty trenches would fill up with water. Medieval building theory was, however, inexact and everyone had different ideas about the depth of foundations, the size of buttresses and so on. Foundations vary greatly from one building to another, apparently bearing little relation to the size and weight of the superstructure. They were often built on the stepped principle, with the greatest width at the base.

The transportation of stone and other building materials by land was slow and costly, so whenever possible they were carried by water. In this fifteenth-century manuscript illustration, a crane is being used to unload large blocks of stone from a barge (Burgerbibliothek, Bern, Mss. hist. helv. I. 16, p. 81).

Building Stone

Most buildings used more than one type of stone because different qualities were needed for different features. Wales has little of the freestone needed for mouldings and window tracery, so most of this had to be imported from Shropshire or, further south, from the quarries of Dundry and Doulting in Somerset, often via Bristol, which was an important port for shipping stone. The polished limestone from the Isle of Purbeck in Dorset was frequently used for decorative enhancement, as in the great tower at Chepstow.

Yet Wales has a fine variety of stones for walling, many of beautiful and unusual colours, and builders used local stone when they could.

The sandstones are especially varied. Red and yellow sandstones were used in St Asaph Cathedral in Flintshire. Purple sandstones include Elwy stone from the river Elwy near St Asaph, and Caerbwdy from Pembrokeshire, which was used extensively at St Davids. The Brecon Beacons in south Wales produce a distinctive red sandstone used at Tretower Court (Breconshire). In Glamorgan, the Pennant Sandstones from the Coal Measures can be any shade from brown through to a silvery grey called 'blue', which first makes an appearance on a grand scale at Caerphilly Castle about 1270.

The imported limestones are creamy white and are often used for tracery and decoration to contrast with a darker stone used for the walls. This is particularly effective at Neath Abbey in Glamorgan. Local limestone — blue lias, which is often shelly — became popular in the fifteenth century and can be seen in the towers at Llandaff Cathedral and St John's Church, Cardiff (Glamorgan).

Many buildings, for example the castles of Conwy and Montgomery (Montgomeryshire), were largely constructed from the rock on which they stand. Conwy Castle is mostly built of the local dark blue grey sandstone, but pink sandstone, brought from the Creuddyn peninsula across the estuary, was used for windows and arrowloops. Later in the fourteenth century, stone was imported from Chester.

Yet the colour of stone was not always important. It was often concealed under paint or whitewash. The grey grandeur of Conwy, which we admire today, was invisible under a coat of sparkling white limewash.

Montgomery Castle (Montgomeryshire) was largely constructed from stone quarried from the rocky hilltop on which it stands.

This elaborate corbel was inserted in the great tower of Chepstow Castle during its remodelling in the second quarter of the thirteenth century. The fine details were beautifully carved in limestones from the quarries at Dundry and Doulting in Somerset, and dark limestone from Purbeck in Dorset and local blue lias were used for decorative enhancement.

Construction and Techniques

Building accounts, useful though they are, do not describe the processes of construction. They record purchases of materials and payments for certain activities. These give us an idea of what materials went into a building and how a result was achieved. For example, a payment to a smith for sharpening tools is an important reminder that stone was sawn or chiselled with metal tools, which rapidly became blunt and needed constant attention. The accounts can have more references to the work going on behind the scenes than to the building itself, but we can often infer what was happening.

The walls were built up in courses. Often, but not invariably, the entire outline of the building was constructed to about 3 feet (1m) in height before work concentrated on one particular area. Churches were usually built from east to west, so that the presbytery or chancel, which was needed for services, could be finished first. Monastic churches, though, could be started on the side next to the monks' living quarters. However, when the abbey church at Tintern was replaced in the late thirteenth century, the monks built the new one around its smaller predecessor to keep the latter in use for as long as possible. Thus, the parts of the present church at Tintern that are next to the cloister went up last.

When a new castle was being built, the priority was to create a defensible enclosure. At Edward I's castle at Harlech, for instance, a building break in the stonework shows that much of the inner ward was initially raised to a height of about 15 feet (4.5m), probably during the first building season in 1283. In succeeding seasons, some of the curtain walls were thickened and the defences were carried to their full height. At Caernarfon, where the walls of Edward I's castle were integrated into the defences of the adjacent new town, a single large enclosure was created during the first period of building. The construction of the northern face of the

Opposite: This fifteenth-century manuscript illustration depicts almost every stage in the construction of a great masonry building, from cutting stone and mixing mortar, through laying walls, to roofing a building and placing a cross atop a finished spire. (Österreichische Nationalbibliothek, Vienna, Cod. 2459, fol. 164).

An artist's impression of Caernarfon in September 1294 during the Welsh rebellion led by Madog ap Llywelyn. After the rebels had overrun the town, they found it easy to take the castle because its northern walls and towers, which looked into the town and were protected by its defences, had not reached full height. After the recovery of the castle, work to complete those fortifications began without delay (Illustration by Ivan Lapper, 1993).

A mason using a plumb-line to check that a wall under construction is vertical, from a mid-thirteenth-century English manuscript illustration (Trinity College Library, Ms. 177 f. 60r — The Board of Trinity College, Dublin).

Although scaffolding sometimes encased a building — as shown in this manuscript illustration painted by the Flemish artist, Gerard Horenbout, about 1500 — it was more commonly put up in smaller sections that were moved as work progressed. This finely executed image also shows centering in place beneath the arch of the doorway and a wooden hoist being used to lift a stone block gripped by large pincers (© British Library Board, Additional Ms. 35313, f. 34).

castle, which looked into the town and was protected by the town walls, proceeded more slowly. After the castle was overrun during the Welsh revolt of 1294–95, the circuit of its own walls and towers was completed as a matter of urgency.

Walls were often very thick: in the twelfth century in particular the walls of a large building were composed of outer faces of dressed ashlar blocks sandwiching a rubble core. Up to a certain height the walls provided a platform for the masons to stand on; and they could go up and down via the staircases and passages that they built into the structure. On small buildings the master mason certainly worked alongside the journeymen, but he also had to supervise the construction and ensure that the rising walls were vertical. For this he used a plumb-line — a ball of lead attached to a string — which was among his personal possessions. He brought his own plumb-line even when the patrons contracted, as they often did, to provide the rest of the tools.

The masons carried loads on their shoulders, protected by thick leather hoods, or in shallow trays carried between two men, or in wheelbarrows. Once the building had risen above one storey the masons raised loads using hoists and pulleys. The stone was either put in a basket or clutched by giant pincers. No medieval hoist survives in Wales, but examples still exist in the English cathedrals of Salisbury and Peterborough: solid oak structures that were left in place should repairs be needed.

When the masons reached the upper levels they put up scaffolding. This was constructed of wooden poles — usually conifer — lashed together with rope or leather thongs. Two thousand scaffolding poles were bought in 1286 for the town walls of Conwy. But scaffolding was expensive and, although some contemporary illustrations show buildings encased in it, it was normally put up in smaller sections and taken down and reused as work moved on. Scaffolding platforms were also cantilevered out from an intermediate point in the elevation to save having to build it up from the ground.

Wales is rich in buildings with surviving putlog holes — holes in the walls that provided anchorage for the horizontal poles that supported the scaffolding walkways. Often they appear in regular horizontal rows, pointing to the use of several levels of staging. However, at the castles of Conwy, Harlech and Beaumaris in north Wales they run up straight walls in diagonal lines or rise in spirals around towers. These putlog holes supported sloping ramps, often made of woven branches, or withies, up which materials were carried or hauled.

Building sites have always been dangerous places. We know from the records that masons fell and injured themselves, and manuscript illuminations show them falling from towers and scaffolding. For safety as well as convenience most of the carving, and even the painting of sculptured details such as roof bosses, was done on the ground before the stones were set in place.

The arrangement of the putlog holes on this tower on Conwy's town walls reveal that its builders used a helicoidal scaffolding ramp that spiralled up around the tower.

Kidwelly Castle seen from across the river Gwendraeth in Carmarthenshire. To the left of the picture, the regular horizontal lines of putlog holes visible on the great gatehouse and the adjoining curtain wall point to the use of several stages of scaffolding during the construction of this part of the castle between about 1390 and 1422.

When setting the carved stones of an arch or other architectural feature in place, masons were guided by setting marks that indicated the correct orientation and sequence. Setting marks and quarry marks should not be confused with another common kind of mark: the mason's mark. A mason's mark is an arrow, a cross, a star or any other kind of simple device that can be chiselled into the stone surface. It was an identification mark, allotted to each mason by the clerk of the works so that, if the masons were doing piecework, each man's contribution could be calculated on payday. Good sequences of these marks can be found at a number of sites in Wales, ranging from Montgomery Castle in the thirteenth century to the gatehouse of Raglan Castle in the 1460s.

Once the walls were completed, the carpenters put on the wooden roof. This protected both the walls and the builders from the weather, and it was only then that any planned stone vaults were built. Vaults were technically the most challenging parts of the building. They had two elements, the webs — or main body of the vault — and the ribs and transverse arches that helped to support them. The ribs and transverse arches were made of dressed stone and put up first; the webs, made of a lighter material, usually rubble, were then built over them.

Any arch — whether in an arcade, a window or a vault — was constructed over a 'form' or centering. This was made of wood or basketwork, shaped to the desired curvature of the arch (p. 13). Traces of the centering are still visible in the undercroft of the bishop's hall at Lamphey in Pembrokeshire. The stonework was mortared in above the centering, and the mortar — a mixture of lime and sand or other aggregate — left to set. Once it had set, which could take days or weeks, and the structure had compressed into rigidity, the centering was dismantled to be used elsewhere. Structural engineers have a 'five-minute rule': if an arch or vault stays up for five minutes after the centering has been taken away, it will stay up for five centuries or more. Medieval buildings provide plenty of evidence that the rule works.

What modern engineers can calculate and test, medieval masons had to learn by experience — hence their tendency to overcompensate with, for example, buttressing. The forces in a stone vault run downwards and outwards. A barrel vault, as at Ewenny Priory, exerts even pressure along the wall. In a groin or rib vault, as at Llandaff Cathedral, the forces run along the cross-shaped creases, and it is where these creases meet the wall that most buttressing is needed. British buildings, with their thick walls and no pretensions to great height, do not normally need the flying

Above: A fifteenth-century mason's mark from the gatehouse of Raglan Castle.

Opposite: The elegant fourteenth-century rib vaults of the chapter house in the Cistercian abbey at Valle Crucis in Denbighshire.

Below left: A barrel vault is a continuous semicircular or pointed tunnel. It exerts even pressure along its supporting walls.

Below middle: A groin vault is created from the intersection of two barrel vaults. The forces are transmitted along the cross-shaped creases   groins   and buttressing may be needed where they meet the walls.

Below right: A rib vault is composed of two elements: the ribs, which are built first and conceal the groins, and the webs, which span the spaces between the ribs and form the main body of the vault. The illustration shows a quadripartite vault, where the ribs divide the vaulting bay into four parts.

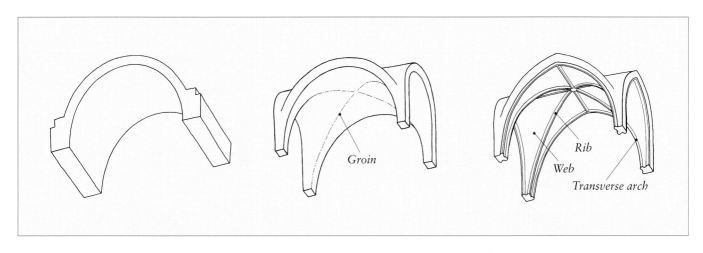

Groin

Rib

Web

Transverse arch

Carreg Cennen Castle stands majestically on a limestone cliff above the river Cennen in Carmarthenshire. The castle's formidable aspect is enhanced by the spur buttresses on its north-east tower, seen here at the right. The spurs supported and protected the tower, but also served as architectural declarations of strength and solidity (Skyscan Balloon Photography, for Cadw).

buttresses that carry the thrusts out over the aisles of large Gothic churches in continental Europe. Yet just as flying buttresses may have been making an aesthetic statement as well as a structural one, so might the buttresses of a castle contain an element of propaganda. The magnificent spur buttresses on towers at Carreg Cennen Castle, Carmarthenshire or the chapel tower at Kidwelly Castle, for example, are as much declarations of power and might as necessary props.

Medieval masons were undoubtedly helped by the stability of their material. Stone acts under compression, so that, in a sense, it props itself up. A vault web is a shell structure and is reinforced by its own curvature. Given adequate foundations, once a stone building has settled and found its equilibrium only an earthquake or a drop in the level of the water table should present any real natural threat.

We are not precisely certain at what stage window tracery was put in, but the setting of the delicate tracery bars may have been delayed until all danger of breakage from accidental falls of masonry was past. It was certainly not until a building had been roofed and vaulted that the glaziers and painters attended to the stained glass and paintwork, just before the scaffolding came down.

The construction of a large and complex building might span years or even decades. When a building site closed down for the winter, unfinished walls had to be weatherproofed: in November 1277 the walls at Builth Castle (Breconshire) were covered in straw, a common form of protection. Seasonal breaks can rarely be detected in a building, but changes in the character of masonry or architectural details often signal more substantial breaks when work resumed after a long interval or under a new master with different ideas. Repairs, too, are detectable, as on the square keep of Dolforwyn Castle (Montgomeryshire), which was damaged in a siege of 1277, and needed strengthening at the corners.

The walls of a finished building were often rendered with lime mortar and/or limewashed, both inside and out. This created a suitable surface for painting on internal walls (see pp. 53–55) and gave external masonry protection from the weather. Such exterior rendering gave White Castle (Monmouthshire) its name in the thirteenth century, and traces are still visible on its walls.

Opposite: An artist's impression of the building of the new abbey church at Tintern in the later thirteenth century, cutaway to show construction details. The main eastern arm of the church is shown with its roof nearly complete, but in the flanking aisle and the south transept the vaults are still being raised. The vault ribs and transverse arches have been inserted but webs have only been completed in the southernmost bay of the transept. The twelfth-century church still stands immediately to the north of the building site so the monks can continue their devotions while construction proceeds (Illustration by Terry Ball, 1990; with modifications, 1995).

The Sculptors

Architectural sculpture added enormously to the cost of building, since carving ornament, foliage and figure sculpture was intricate and time-consuming. Sculpture also required good quality freestone, which often had to be brought from some distance. Building accounts and bills for wages reflect the time and money spent on enhancing buildings with sculptured decoration. Yet the record of an image bought in Chester in 1286 for the castle chapel at Conwy shows that not all sculpture was worked at the site.

Decorative carving was done by masons, some of whom may have specialized in it. It was only in the later Middle Ages, however, that dedicated figure sculptors — *imagiers* — appear in lists of wages. In any case, much ornamental sculpture was an extension of the architecture itself, not only in the form of capitals, corbels and the like, but also in such works as the early thirteenth-century niche in St Illtyd's Church, Llantwit Major (Glamorgan), where the foliage of a Tree of Jesse — a popular medieval image depicting the ancestry of Christ — is carved among the mouldings. Since even figure sculpture is intimately linked to architectural structure, always placed in a niche or against a wall, the distinction between architecture and sculpture is not as clear as it might seem. The great hall at Caerphilly Castle, for example, has ballflower carved in relief in the mouldings around the windows, and the wooden ceiling (now modern) is supported by stone corbels, each consisting of three carved heads. The close relationship between architecture

Above: This early thirteenth-century niche in St Illtyd's Church in Llantwit Major (Glamorgan) is surrounded by an intricately carved Tree of Jesse. As in this instance, much ornamental sculpture in the Middle Ages was an extension of the architecture itself (ffotograff).

Opposite: One of the vigorously carved thirteenth-century capitals in the nave of St Mary's Church, Haverfordwest.

Left: A sculptor greets his patron in this detail from a manuscript illustration painted by the French artist, Jean Colombe, after 1490. The sculptor's tools, including various chisels and punches, lie on the ground ready for use (Bildarchiv Preussischer Kulturbesitz/ Kupferstichkabinett, Staatliche Museen zu Berlin, Min. 4645/ Jörg P. Anders).

Opposite: The close relationship between sculpture and architecture is evident at St Winifred's Well in Holywell (Flintshire). The fifteenth-century well chamber at this important pilgrimage site is covered by a richly ornamented vault. Elaborate keystones mark the junctions of the finely moulded vault ribs and scenes of the life of St Winifred and her uncle, St Beuno, decorate the central pendant keystone seen in the centre top of the view.

Left: A meticulous reconstruction of the Tintern Abbey pulpitum based on surviving fragments. This early fourteenth-century screen stood at the eastern end of the abbey church's nave and was richly decorated with micro-architecture and other ornament (After S. A. Harrison, R. K. Morris and D. M. Robinson, 'A Fourteenth-Century Pulpitum Screen at Tintern Abbey, Monmouthshire', The Antiquaries Journal 78 [1998]; drawing by Chris Jones-Jenkins).

and sculpture can be seen even more vividly in the fifteenth-century stone vault over St Winifred's Well. Elaborate foliate keystones mark the junctions between the main and subsidiary ribs. The main ribs converge on a central, pendant keystone carved with scenes of the lives of St Winifred and her uncle, Saint Beuno.

Architectural historians use foliage sculpture and window tracery, along with the mouldings of piers and arches, to date undocumented buildings and to identify the likely origins of the masons. The upright, stiff-leaf foliage capitals (see p. 39) and multi-shafted piers from the church of Cwmhir Abbey (Radnorshire) — now removed to the parish church at Llanidloes (Montgomeryshire) — show that the nave was built in the thirteenth century by a group drawn from the west Midlands. The building stone — Grinshill Sandstone — is from Shropshire in the same general area (p. 24).

Sculpture was not confined to the architectural elements. Many church furnishings were carved in stone: altar screens, sedilia (seats for the clergy beside the altar), niches and fonts. These required delicate skills in carving. Screens often demanded intricate work in micro-architecture, such as miniature pinnacles and battlements, very fine mouldings and repetitive ornament, such as square tablet flowers, and other motifs applied to mouldings and stringcourses. The fourteenth-century altar screen at Llantwit Major is a good example of such delicate work. So too is the early fourteenth-century pulpitum screen that once stood in the nave of the abbey church at Tintern: the fragmentary remains of the pulpitum reveal fine examples of micro-architecture and other ornament, possibly designed by the West Country master mason, William Joy.

Late medieval effigies were often produced by masons who specialized in their production. Just as on this effigy of Sir William Hastings (d. about 1349) in St Mary's Church, Abergavenny (Monmouthshire), details of dress, armour and other accoutrements could be rendered in great detail.

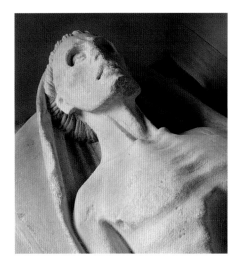

The cadaver effigy thought to commemorate John Denby or Tynby (d. 1499) in St Mary's Church, Tenby in Pembrokeshire.

In the later Middle Ages, the carving of tomb effigies became an important branch of sculpture. Master masons set up as tomb makers and provided both the effigy and the tomb chest upon which it rested. By the fourteenth century effigies were carved almost in the round. They were usually made from blocks of freestone at least 6 feet (1.8m) long, 2 feet (0.6m) wide and 18 inches (0.5m) deep. Work on an effigy proceeded like that on any stone sculpture. The sculptor used trimming hammers and chisels to rough out the figure; surface detail and undercutting were added with gouges and punches. Finally the effigy was smoothly finished and sometimes rubbed with emery to a high polish.

Despite the fact that effigies and statues were often to be plastered and painted, dress was rendered in great detail. The sculptor of the priest's effigy, dating from the fourteenth century, in St Cedwyn's Church, Llangedwyn (Denbighshire) depicted his vestments very accurately; and the armour of Sir William Hastings (d. around 1349) in St Mary's Church, Abergavenny (Monmouthshire) is rendered with equal care. In the late fourteenth and fifteenth centuries, when it became fashionable to be shown not in the prime of life, but in the decay of death, sculptors had to exercise their talents on skeletons and shrouds to make so-called cadaver effigies, like that thought to be John Denby or Tynby, archdeacon of St Davids (d.1499), at St Mary's Church in Tenby (Pembrokeshire).

The tomb chest could be used to display heraldry and religious imagery. The mid-fifteenth-century tomb chest of the patron of Raglan Castle, Sir William ap Thomas (d. 1445), and his wife Gwladus (d. 1454) at Abergavenny, depicts a scene of the Annunciation to the Virgin, set in three sections under architectural canopies.

The master mason would also create the setting for a tomb. At St Davids Cathedral, for instance, the master accommodated the tomb of Bishop Henry de Gower (d. 1347) within the design for the pulpitum screen. If a tomb was set in a wall niche, he would design the arch mouldings. These mouldings could be elaborate, as on the late fourteenth-century tomb of Dafydd ap Hywel ap Madog in Tremeirchion parish church (Flintshire), which is fringed with ornamental double cusping.

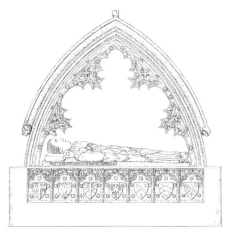

The master mason who designed the tomb of Dafydd ap Hywel ap Madog in the church of Corpus Christi, Tremeirchion (Flintshire), framed it with elaborate mouldings ornamented with double cusping — drawing from Colin A. Gresham, Medieval Stone Carving in North Wales *(Cardiff: University of Wales Press, 1968).*

The fourteenth-century pulpitum screen at St Davids Cathedral (Pembrokeshire) was designed to accommodate the tomb of Bishop Henry de Gower (d. 1347), which is visible through the elaborately embellished arch to the right.

Above: An early thirteenth-century stiff-leaf capital from the nave of Llandaff Cathedral, near Cardiff (Glamorgan).

Left: Exuberant stiff-leaf decorates the capital of the central pier of the chapter house at Margam Abbey, which was probably built between around 1203 and 1213. The deeply undercut foliage testifies to the skill of the mason who carved it.

Stiff-Leaf Foliage

Stiff-leaf is a very beautiful carved foliage design that first appeared in the late twelfth century and continued in use until after the middle of the thirteenth.

Stiff-leaf was used mostly on capitals, with a particularly striking effect when the capitals were grouped together on a clustered pier. The core of the capital is an inverted bell shape. Against this core upstanding leaf stems culminate in a frothy bunch of stylized leaves, sometimes bending outwards, sometimes sideways. Small animals or human heads often poke out among the leaves.

In the nave of Llandaff Cathedral, the thirteenth-century stiff-leaf is very like the famous carved foliage at Wells Cathedral in Somerset. The stems are carved in distinct relief, moving slightly off vertical, and the burst of leaves, which bunches over like a fist, is deeply and delicately undercut.

The early thirteenth-century piers that were once in the abbey church at Cwmhir are now in Llanidloes parish church (p. 24). The clustered columns are topped with frothing stiff-leaf that is blown a little sideways. The stems and leaves are coarser than at Llandaff, and the lobed formation of the leaves is more pronounced.

These lobes become more prominent in later stiff-leaf, as in the nave of St Mary's Church in Haverfordwest (p. 34). Here the foliage rambles round the capitals, much interrupted by animals, mythical creatures and human heads. These are carved with less skill than the leaves, which suggests that the sculptor was trained primarily to carve foliage. A particularly charming motif is a monkey playing a pipe.

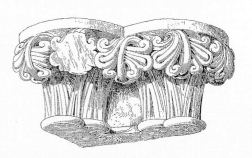

Above: An antiquarian drawing of a stiff-leaf capital excavated at Cwmhir Abbey. After the abbey's suppression in the sixteenth century, part of the nave arcade with its fine stiff-leaf capitals was moved to the church of St Idloes in Llanidloes. The drawing, by Worthington G. Smith, was published in The Transactions of the Honourable Society of Cymmrodorion, *1894–95 (Library, National Museum of Wales).*

The Carpenters

In ordinary medieval life, timber buildings were the norm and stone the exception. Wood was prized above stone by patrons and by poets. What the French poet, Guillaume de Lorris, did for stone masons in *The Romance of the Rose* (p. 11), Welsh poets did for carpenters. Rhys Goch Eryri praised the new hall or court (*llys*) at Penrhyn, near Caernarfon, in a poem composed sometime after 1405. He described it as built of oak and better than the grey stone of Caernarfon Castle. He was almost certainly making a political point, that Welsh wood was better than English stone; but Welsh poets also celebrated wood for its own qualities. They even used wood and the carpenter's craft as metaphors: the Glamorgan poet, Iorwerth Fynglwyd (d. 1527), described himself as 'a full carpenter of the poetic measure'. Although carpenters produced spectacular timber work for stone buildings, they came into their own with wooden ones.

Carpenters were ubiquitous, but because wood is perishable only a fraction of their work survives, though much is hidden behind later stone cladding. We know little about their professional organization. Structural carpenters were often itinerant; joiners, who made furniture, usually stayed in their own workshops. Timber was delivered to them and they emerged to fit such fixed pieces as church screens or choir stalls.

Carpenters provided essential support for other crafts, making, for example, scaffolding, centering for arches, hoists, ladders and tools for masons. They made vehicles for transporting materials, such as carts and wheelbarrows; and shipwrights built the boats that ferried the stone along the waterways. On a grander scale their work included timber-framed houses, some of which, like Bryndraenog in Radnorshire, were large structures. They also built industrial structures, such as windmills like the one that appears in the wall painting in the church of St Saeran at Llanynys, Denbighshire (see p. 55). A wood carver could also make figures, like the effigy of Sir John Hastings (d. 1325) in the church of St Mary at Abergavenny, or, in the same church, the huge wooden statue of Jesse, which is all that remains of a monumental late medieval Tree of Jesse.

Noah depicted as a contemporary carpenter with the tools of his trade in an English manuscript illustration of around 1420–30 (Bodleian Library, University of Oxford, Ms. Barlow 53 [R]).

Opposite: A timber screen at Tretower Court (Breconshire), built in the late fifteenth century. Even when a building had stone walls, carpenters played an essential role in the construction, not only by fashioning tools, hoists and the centering for arches, but also by framing roofs and constructing internal fittings.

The well-preserved wooden Jesse figure in St Mary's Church, Abergavenny. Once part of a monumental fifteenth-century Tree of Jesse, this is one of the finest pieces of medieval sculpture in Britain and still retains traces of the paint that enlivened it.

A mid-sixteenth-century carpenter proudly carved his tools on this bracket at Old Impton in Radnorshire.

Few medieval carpenters' tools survive in Wales, although a felling axe was found at Harlech. But at Old Impton, a mid-sixteenth-century house in Radnorshire, the carpenter carved a set of his tools in low relief on a bracket of the timber-framed porch. They include a hatchet for cutting and trimming; a saw; a draw-knife for trimming; an adze for smoothing the wood; an auger, a chisel and a morticing axe for making joints; and a square and dividers. Carpenters were almost certainly trained to use these tools in the forests, on building sites and in places where timber frames were assembled.

The forest was the equivalent of the quarry in that the master carpenter went there to choose the timber and mark the trees for felling. Parts of Wales were richly forested with both wild and managed woodlands. Trees were coppiced — periodically cut back to ground level — for smaller pieces, but well-grown specimens were needed for large beams. Structural timber was almost always oak, and the forests of Brecon in Breconshire and Ewloe in Flintshire were an abundant source until the sixteenth century, when increased charcoal burning reduced them. When the castles of Beaumaris and Caernarfon were being built, carpenters were sent to the Gwynedd woodlands in the Conwy valley to fell trees and prepare large joists and other pieces of timber. In June 1320, Walter 'le Bordhewer' of Llanrwst (Denbighshire) was paid 20s. for twelve big joists, each 18 feet (5.5m) long, for the great hall over the gate at Caernarfon Castle. Timber was also brought in large quantities from England.

The wood was used when it was newly felled and green, so that it seasoned after it was put in place. After felling, the sawyers cut the tree into beams, using two-handed saws over a pit or with a trestle; the beams were then carted or shipped to the building site.

The initial site was not necessarily the final destination. Although timber structures could be very complex, they were generally constructed from components — wall frames and roof trusses — that could be prefabricated and this often seems to have taken place in special areas some distance away from the eventual construction site.

The individual timbers were set out with compasses and squares, as in masonry. They were measured and cut, and the frame or truss was then assembled on the ground. If all was satisfactory, the timbers were marked with chalk or inscribed with setting and position marks before they were taken apart for transport. When the timbers arrived at the site for final assembly, the marks enabled the carpenters to know where each piece should go. It was in fact a more elaborate version of modern self-assembly kits, some evidence of which survives at Tretower Court.

Opposite: The artist who produced this illustration for the Bedford Hours *between 1414 and 1423 imagined Noah's Ark as a substantial timber-framed building of his own time. Carpenters often prefabricated frames and trusses for such buildings at some distance from the final construction site (© British Library Board, Additional Ms. 18850, f. 15v).*

Right: Sawyers cutting timber with a two-handed saw in a manuscript illustration produced in England about 1340 (© British Library Board, Royal 10 E. IV, f. 99v).

Coment noe seg comenca a noel fair vne arce et y metre vne paire de toutes les bestes pour le deluge

A general view of the nave of St Ishow's Church, Partrishow (Breconshire) showing the late fifteenth-century timber barrel or wagon roof and the breathtaking rood screen and loft of about 1500.

Virtually every element of the rood loft at Partrishow is embellished with sumptuous carving. The numbers refer to features discussed in the text. The loft would originally have been surmounted by the rood — carved figures of the crucified Christ, flanked by the Virgin Mary and St John.

Partrishow Screen

Many church furnishings, including the wooden screens dividing the nave from the chancel, have been destroyed, either during the upheavals of the Reformation and the Civil War or as a result of changing fashions in later centuries. What has survived has often been heavily restored. An almost complete example of a screen with a loft above survives in the small church at Bettws Newydd in Monmouthshire. Two elaborate, but restored, screens can be seen in the church of St Jerome at Llangwm Uchaf (Monmouthshire) and in the church of St Ishow at Partrishow in Breconshire. They show the full glory of elaborate late fifteenth-century screens in Wales.

Partrishow stands isolated on a remote hillside near the healing well of St Ishow (Issui) in the Black Mountains. Inside the tiny church, the magnificent oak screen dominates the nave. In front of it, two rare examples of stone altars survive facing the nave. These were used for offerings and prayers for the dead. The screen has plain panels — wainscot — at its base, with openings above. These are topped by delicate openwork tracery, which creates 'windows' through to the chancel.

Above the screen the loft projects towards the congregation in the nave. It is supported on a long beam — the bressumer [1] — which is carved with three different designs of leaf scroll, all deeply undercut. The uppermost is a vine scroll that issues from the mouth of a dragon. Above this is more openwork tracery divided by thick, moulded muntins [2] decorated with miniature buttresses in imitation of stonework. The headbeam [3], above the tracery, is carved with undulating wavy lines and its top edge is drilled with some small holes for candles. The back of the screen, tucked under the chancel arch, is quite plain, and unlike most screens, this one was never painted.

Screen lofts had two main purposes: they displayed the rood — carved figures of the crucified Christ, the Virgin Mary and St John — and supported singers and perhaps a small, portable organ. The loft at Partrishow is lit by a small window, and a flight of stone stairs provided access.

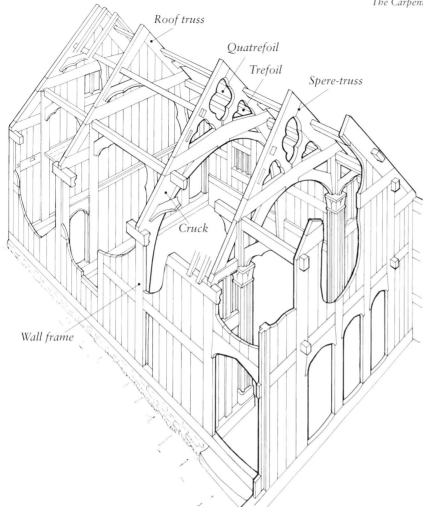

Roof truss

Quatrefoil

Trefoil

Spere-truss

Cruck

Wall frame

This cutaway drawing of the fifteenth-century house at Pen-y-bryn, near Llansilin in Denbighshire, illustrates how crucks could be incorporated in a building that also used frames and trusses. The timber work at Pen-y-bryn includes a spere-truss, which was used to mark the division between the hall and the screens passage that provided access to the entrance of the house and the various service rooms (Royal Commission on the Ancient and Historical Monuments of Wales).

Below: At St Collen's Church in Llangollen (Denbighshire), a fine hammer-beam roof is combined with an intricately carved panelled ceiling.

Timbers were usually joined together by mortice-and-tenon joints. Carpenters occasionally used dovetailing and made scarf joints for joining two lengths of timber. They hardly ever used iron nails for structural timber, fixing joints instead with wooden pegs.

From the fourteenth century through to the sixteenth, many Welsh hall houses were built with crucks. A cruck is a pair of curved timbers, or blades, cut from the same oak tree and stood together to form an arch with a wide base. The use of crucks to frame a house created an open, undivided space. Crucks are documented in Wales at Harlech in 1306, but they can also be dated by dendrochronology (tree-ring dating), which gives a felling date: the elaborate timber work at Bryndraenog, for example, was made from trees felled in 1436. Crucks could be combined with other timber work, as at Pen-y-bryn, near Llansilin in Denbighshire, a fifteenth-century house that has crucks as well as frames and trusses.

The timbers at Pen-y-bryn are decorated with openwork quatrefoils and trefoils. In structural carpentry ornament is generally at its best in church furnishings and late medieval wooden ceilings. The church of St Mary at Cilcain in Flintshire, has a fine hammer-beam roof and at St Collen's Church in Llangollen (Denbighshire), hammer beams combine with a panelled ceiling carved with tracery, foliage, mythical beasts and filigree. Modern scholars have equated the intricate patterns made by carpenters in medieval Wales with the words composed by contemporary poets.

The Tilers

In 1448 the works organization at Newport Castle bought 18,000 roof slates from a Cornishman, Auncell Wyke, and 24 ceramic ridge tiles from Alfred Crocker of Cardiff. Like all ceramics, the ridge tiles were made of fired clay. Decorated floor tiles were made of the same material. Floor tiles have been found at many sites in Wales, both domestic and ecclesiastical. Churches and palaces had glazed tile floors by the middle of the thirteenth century; by the fifteenth, wealthy townspeople were using tiles in place of beaten earth or rush-strewn floors. Floor tiles were, however, most popular in the parts of Wales most open to English influence and trade.

The styles of decoration can be related to well-established centres of tile manufacture in south-west England, the Severn Valley and Chester. Although tiles were imported through Chester, Bristol and Shrewsbury, a tile kiln has been found at Denbigh (Denbighshire), and there is evidence that tiles of English type were also made in Wales. Some late twelfth- or early thirteenth-century tiles at the Carmarthenshire abbeys of Whitland and Talley may be the work of immigrant French craftsmen. However, we know little about the organization of the craft and no names of individual tilers have come down to us. Records use the words 'tiler' and 'paviour' indiscriminately to denote makers of roof and floor tiles, and those who set the tiles in place.

Tile making, like much of the building industry, was a seasonal occupation. The clay was dug in the autumn and left exposed to the weather until the spring, having been turned at least once during the winter. The winter rains helped to refine the clay by washing out some impurities, but further processing seems to have been limited to the removal of obvious large stones by hand. Grit or sand might be added to prevent the tiles from cracking while they were being fired. The tiles themselves were made and fired in the summer.

Mosaic tiles, which were among the earliest types of decorative paving tiles, were formed in a range of rectilinear or curved shapes, cut with a template from a flat sheet of clay. Later tiles were a more convenient square shape. They were made by pummelling and hammering the clay into an open wooden mould and smoothed with a wet scraper to leave a finer surface. Once removed from the mould, the edges were bevelled so that the tiles would line up evenly when laid on the floor. The tiles were then dried for several days in open-sided sheds.

When the tiles were 'leather hard', they were decorated and glazed. They were generally either plain glazed or decorated with incised or stamped patterns. The most common ornament, seen in tiles from Tintern, was a stamped pattern with the sunken areas filled in — inlaid — with white clay. White clay could also be used in liquid form as a slip over the whole surface, as on the early mosaic tiles at Basingwerk Abbey (Flintshire). Another common type, used in the

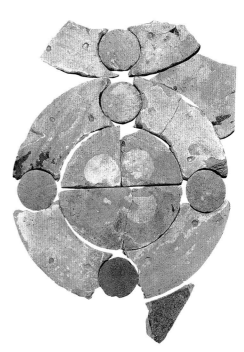

Mid-thirteenth-century mosaic tiles from Basingwerk Abbey in Flintshire (National Museum of Wales).

Opposite: Tile making in a detail from a Flemish manuscript illustration of the middle of the fifteenth century (© British Library Board, Additional Ms. 38122, f. 78v).

A beautifully preserved inlaid tile from Strata Marcella Abbey in Montgomeryshire. The tile could have formed part of a larger design (Powysland Museum, Welshpool, A247-A255).

fourteenth-century pavements at Strata Florida Abbey, was the line-impressed tile, where a linear design filled the surface and was then left plain or coated in a slip. In the second half of the thirteenth century, Whitland Abbey and Haverfordwest Priory had some tiles with the pattern standing out in relief, a reversal of the sunken method. Relief tiles are uncomfortable to walk on and therefore less common.

The last stage before firing was adding the glaze, which would bond with the clay to produce a hard-wearing surface. The glaze was lead, probably made by heating lead scrap in a furnace until it became ash of lead oxide. The ash was either brushed on to the surface of the tile or applied mixed in a liquid — often ale. During firing the lead oxide combined with silica and alumina present in the clay itself.

Tiles were glazed in a range of colours. Iron, present in the clay or in the iron tools used by the tilers, always leached into the glaze, so that the glaze over a white clay slip would look yellow. If the tiles were brown the glaze looked red. Reducing the oxygen in the kiln would make the tiles grey and the glaze a dull green; copper could also be added to produce a more vivid green, and adding more copper or brass created a black glaze.

All kinds of tile, whether they were for roofs or floors, were fired in the same way. The kiln ovens were built over barrel-vaulted brick chambers, in which wood was burned. The tiles were placed on end, not touching, and stacked so that an unglazed surface faced a glazed one. The tiles were dried at a lower initial temperature and then fired for two days at temperatures approaching 1,000 degrees Celsius.

Above: An artist's reconstruction of the late fourteenth-century tile kiln that was excavated at Denbigh in Denbighshire (National Museum of Wales).

Opposite: Four identical line-impressed tiles were used to create each of the roundels in this early fourteenth-century pavement from Strata Florida Abbey.

Above: A relief tile from Whitland Abbey in Carmarthenshire (Carmarthenshire County Museum, 1976.809).

The exotic motifs that appear on many 'Wessex school' tiles were ultimately derived from eastern textiles, like this ninth-century Byzantine fabric decorated with a bird in a medallion (The Art Archive/Abbaye de Saint Foy Conques/ Gianni Dagli Orti).

Wessex School Tiles

The interiors of many medieval buildings, even austere Cistercian abbey churches, were enhanced by patterned, glazed floor tiles. One of the most widespread types of medieval tile was the inlaid tile, which produced a two-colour effect. The pattern was pressed well into wet clay and the sunk areas filled in with white clay. When it was dry the tiler scraped the surplus white from the surface, leaving a clear light-on-dark pattern. This was then lead glazed and fired in the kiln.

A famous set of inlaid tiles was made in 1250–51 for the royal palace at Clarendon in Wiltshire. Evidence of the king's tilers has also come from the cathedrals at Winchester and Salisbury, creating a style that has come to be known as the 'Wessex school'. Its distinguishing characteristics can all be traced to the Clarendon designs and their influence can be found widely in south Wales from the mid-thirteenth until the early fourteenth century at sites ranging from Monmouth Priory (Monmouthshire) and Chepstow Castle in the east to Kidwelly Castle, Whitland Abbey and St Non's Chapel, St Davids, in the west.

We can detect the Clarendon influence in tiles from Tintern Abbey. Designs are set inside a circle, which is embellished with fleur-de-lis points projecting into the corners of the square tile. Inside the circle are various exotic motifs: symmetrical, stylized leaf patterns and heraldic creatures such as lions and griffins.

All these motifs were derived from woven silk textiles that were brought from the East through Constantinople, Venice and Sicily. Such silks were much prized and often made up into church vestments or held in treasuries.

These inlaid tiles from Tintern Abbey date from the late thirteenth to the early fourteenth centuries. The influence of the Clarendon tiles is particularly clear in the tile on the lower right, where a symmetrical foliage pattern is enclosed within a circle ornamented with fleur-de-lis points in the corners (National Museum of Wales).

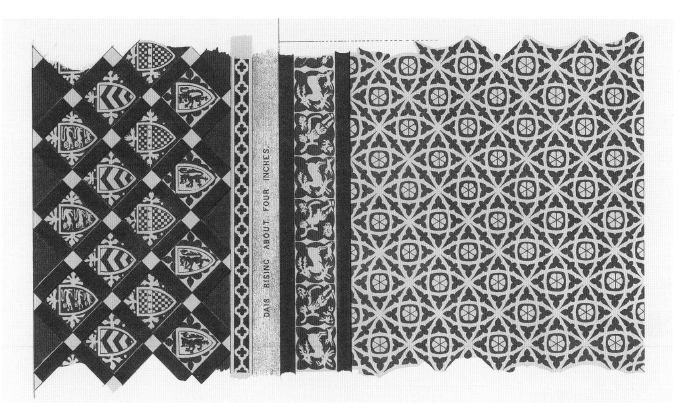

DAIS RISING ABOUT FOUR INCHES.

When the tiles were ready to be laid, the paviours made a bed of lime mortar into which they set them. Mosaic tiles are very attractive to look at, but not very adaptable, so when a large floor area was to be covered with a pattern, square tiles came into their own. They could be set in alternating plain colours, or patterns with plain borders. Some tiles have a single motif, like the lions, griffins and foliage designs at Tintern Abbey; but each could form part of a larger, elaborate design that covered up to sixty-four tiles. Part of such a floor was found at Neath Abbey. Here, a central circle, which extended over sixteen tiles, was contained within a quatrefoil, which itself lay within a scalloped rectangle so that the whole design covered sixty-four tiles. The four tiles in the centre of the circle were decorated with shields of arms and surrounded by composite patterns of curved motifs resembling stone tracery. Grotesques, or lion's heads, featured in the corners of the design. This big square was flanked by sets of sixteen tiles showing variants on the main circular motif. The tracery, foliage and shields of arms on the tiles probably reflected the decoration of the church itself.

The tiles discovered in Wales display many different design techniques. The cloister of Haverfordwest Priory had a chequered pattern. Strata Marcella Abbey, near Welshpool (Montgomeryshire), had plain glazed tiles with an impressed linear pattern and no white slip. Among the designs made popular in the fifteenth century by the manufactory at Great Malvern in Worcestershire were architectural elements spread over a large number of individual pieces. These inspired other workshops in the Severn Valley area, one of which produced the tiles that were laid at the east end of St Davids Cathedral around 1500. There are heraldic tiles of Malvern design in the chapel of Raglan Castle; such tiles were so popular that they were also made in a kiln at Monmouth.

A print published by H. H. Knight around 1848 (Specimens of Inlaid Tiles … from Neath Abbey) *recording one of the impressive mid-fourteenth-century pavements of inlaid tiles then still* in situ *at Neath Abbey (Glamorgan).*

Among the designs made popular by the tile manufactory at Great Malvern (Worcestershire) in the fifteenth century were architectural motifs spread over a number of individual pieces. This tile was found with others carrying Malvern-inspired designs during the excavation of a kiln in Monmouth (Nelson Museum and Local History Centre).

The Painters

Medieval buildings did not display the large areas of bare stone and wood that we see today. Most were at least limewashed white inside and often outside as well, and many were highly and elaborately coloured from an early date. The great tower of Chepstow Castle has traces of colour in the late eleventh-century wall niches.

In Wales there are remains of extensive figured schemes, such as that formerly in the church of St Teilo, at Llandeilo Tal-y-bont, near Swansea (Glamorgan) — now preserved in St Fagans National History Museum, near Cardiff. Wall paintings of Christ, the saints and other religious subjects would have been familiar sights in the churches of medieval Wales. These and other images in stained glass, sculpture and church fittings would have quickened the faith of all viewers, but they also helped the priest to communicate fundamental doctrines to the illiterate populace.

Even non-figured decoration could be complex. Whitened walls could be lined with red-painted lines in imitation of masonry. Sometimes, stencilled motifs were applied to this fictive masonry: sunbursts appear in a window of Marshal's Tower at Chepstow. The painted ashlar in the bishop's palace at Lamphey and the chapel of nearby Manorbier Castle (Pembrokeshire) is decorated with rosettes. In the later of two decorative schemes at Ewenny Priory the lines marking the blocks of masonry were decorated with alternate cinquefoils and flowers. The painters at Ewenny also created

Above: An extensive series of late medieval wall paintings was revealed in the church of St Teilo at Llandeilo Tal-y-bont (Glamorgan), now in St Fagans National History Museum, near Cardiff. This striking scene shows the mocking of Christ (Royal Commission on the Ancient and Historical Monuments of Wales).

Opposite: An exciting discovery of well-preserved late medieval wall paintings has recently been made at St Cadoc's Church, Llancarfan (Glamorgan). Parts of an impressive scene of St George battling the dragon, including this striking princess, have begun to emerge from beneath thick layers of limewash.

Left: A reconstruction of the second decorative scheme at the east end of the priory church at Ewenny. The thirteenth-century painters decorated the fictive masonry with cinquefoils and flowers and even created illusory columns flanking the eastern windows (© Sophie Stewart: Paine and Stewart).

Above: Painters decorating walls or vaults frequently needed scaffolding, as shown in this detail from a mid-thirteenth-century manuscript of the Cantigas de Santa Maria *(© Patrimonio Nacional/El Escorial, Madrid, Ms. T.I.1, fol 109r).*

Above right: When the comfortable apartments in Marten's Tower at Chepstow Castle were built in the 1290s, their walls were painted in a striking scheme using red fictive masonry and extensive areas of yellow ochre as shown in this reconstruction (Illustration by Bevis Sale, 2001; with modifications, 2008).

A painter mixing his colours, shown in an English manuscript illustration of 1360–75 (© British Library Board, Royal 6 E. VI, f. 329).

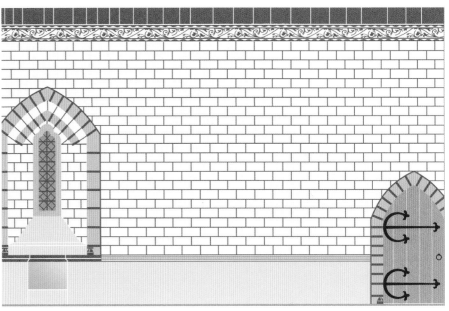

such fictive architectural details as columns flanking the east windows. Walls were not always white: the colour scheme for Marten's Tower at Chepstow in the 1290s included red masonry lining on a pale yellow ochre ground. At St Davids in the 1330s, Bishop Henry de Gower painted the exterior walls of his palace a deep, warm red, making bold colour contrasts with the purple Caerbwdy stone used for much of the decorative sculpture, and the chequerboard patterning of the parapet.

Painters were itinerant, and worked mainly in small businesses consisting of a master and perhaps one or two assistants. The only painter in medieval Wales whom we know by name is one Stephen the Painter, who decorated a chamber at Rhuddlan Castle, where Edward I stayed over Christmas in 1283. The records of both Savoy and Westminster mention a painter called Stephen: if this man is the same one, he had a distinguished and exotic career, like his mason colleague, James of St George (p. 8).

Although the keystones of vaults were painted before they were set in place, the walls were painted and the windows glazed only after the difficult and dangerous building process was complete. In northern Europe painters did not use the Italian method of applying the paint on fresh wet plaster (fresco). Instead, they worked on a dry surface, or ground (secco). The ground could be a lime render or limewash applied direct to the stonework; a good example of the use of both grounds has been identified at Ewenny Priory. The master then set up a preparatory grid on the wall using a chalked string snapped against the plaster for the painters to follow. The painters made outline drawings of the design in red chalk or sometimes by light incisions.

The painters prepared all the paints and materials themselves. The apprentices ground the pigments, which were bound with a tempera medium such as egg. Alternatively, the ground was primed with a lead white and the pigments bound with an oil medium, such as linseed. Oil painting was common in medieval Britain from at least the thirteenth century for both wall and panel paintings. Palettes were made of wood or even shell, and stencils for applied patterns were cut from sheets of lead. Paint brushes were made of squirrel's or hog's hair. A wide range of colours could be used, but even those schemes that were based on red and yellow ochres with some black and white could have rich, vivid effects.

Wall Painting

In the north aisle of the church of
St Saeran, Llanynys, Denbighshire, there
is a fifteenth-century wall painting
of St Christopher, patron saint of
travellers and protector from sudden
death. The giant figure of the saint looks
up at the Christ Child whom he carries
across the river. Christ's right hand is
raised in a blessing and in the other
hand he holds an orb, representing the
world. The water is alive with fish.
There is a timber windmill on the left
bank of the river and on the right a
bearded hermit holds up a lamp to
guide the saint.

For such a large painting — 12 feet
(3.7m) by 9 feet (2.8m) — the painter
would have needed a wooden scaffold.
He would have set guidelines on the
plaster using string and then drawn the
design with chalk before applying the
paint to dry plaster. The painting was
executed using a tempera medium in
which the paint pigment was bound
with egg, or perhaps size or limewater.

The colours are mostly earth
colours, shades of ochre, red earth
and burnt ochres. Green verdigris,
which is derived from copper, is
used for the sprouting branches of
Christopher's staff and for his cloak.
Christ's halo is picked out in gold.
The repeated monogram of the Virgin
Mary that decorates the background
was probably applied through a stencil
cut from lead sheeting.

The style here closely resembles
the painting on the chancel arch of
St Giles, Wrexham, and may be by
the same artist.

*The wall painting of St Christopher
in the church of St Saeran, Llanynys
(Denbighshire) is so large that the artist
would have needed to work from a
scaffold (ffotograff).*

The Glaziers

The glass painter, Gerlachus, is portrayed holding a brush and a pot of paint in a window of about 1160 from the German monastery of Arnstein (Sonia Halliday/ Laura Lushington).

Although wall painting can be very striking, in medieval times stained glass was valued much more highly. So much glass has been damaged that this can be difficult to appreciate today, and records of individual glaziers are scarce. Just as we know the name of one wall painter working in Wales, so we have the name of one glazier: Simon, who worked at Caernarfon Castle in 1283. Yet stained glass involved the two elements that medieval people most admired in a craft: highly skilled workmanship and the effect of jewelled colour. Although stained glass was used in very high-class secular buildings it was far more common in churches. Most surviving examples in Wales date from the late fourteenth century onwards.

White glass was made in England, but coloured glass was imported at great expense from northern Europe and Venice. Glass was made in areas with beech woods, which provided not only timber for firing the kilns, but also the essential ingredients of glass — sand (silica) and the beech wood itself. Beech yielded the potash that lowered the melting point of the sand. The glass makers produced colours by adding oxides of metals such as manganese, cobalt or copper to the molten glass. This was done in clay pots, so this type of glass is known as pot-metal

Opposite: Various stages in the production of glass are shown in this manuscript illustration of about 1410 (© British Library Board, Additional Ms. 24189, f. 16).

Below: Two panels from a window of 1498 depicting scenes from the life of St Anne and her daughter, the Virgin Mary, in the church of All Saints, Gresford in Denbighshire (ffotograff).

This fourteenth-century roundel of the Virgin Mary in the church of St Mary at Treuddyn in Flintshire is an early example of the use of pot-metal glass in Wales (ffotograff).

glass. The roundel showing the Virgin Mary in the church of St Mary at Treuddyn in Flintshire is an early example in Wales of the use of pot-metal glass. Red glass required special treatment because the colour was so intense at normal thickness that it looked almost black and cut out too much light. To solve this problem, a thin slice of red glass could be interleaved with white (flashing), or coated very thinly on to the surface of white glass. The late fifteenth-century scenes of the Virgin Mary at Gresford show how this method balanced the reds with the other colours in the picture.

In the later period the taste for heavily saturated, glowing colours gave way to lighter hues amid areas of white glass, which allowed more light into the building. White glass and new procedures for painting and firing produced alternatives to pot-metal glass, though the different techniques were often combined. Glaziers painted vitreous enamels on to white glass, and produced yellow-stain by painting silver nitrate on the outside of white glass and firing it at various temperatures. The mid-fifteenth-century Crucifixion panel in the church of St Mary, Llanllugan (Montgomeryshire), demonstrates the effects of these new techniques, which altered the brightness of church buildings and proved popular in secular ones.

The small, diamond-shaped panes known as quarries, which were the cheapest to produce, combined yellow-stain and paint to make stylized foliage designs on white glass. These survive in many places, but the early sixteenth-century church of St Meugan at Llanrhudd (Denbighshire) has particularly delightful quarries depicting oak sprigs complete with acorns.

The glaziers controlled the entire process of creating a stained-glass window, even making the lead strips that joined the pieces of glass together, and supervising the manufacture of the iron armatures that held the window in place. Originally, they drew out the design full-scale on a whitewashed surface. In the later Middle Ages,

Right: This Crucifix in St Mary's Church, Llanllugan (Montgomeryshire), illustrates the use of yellow-stain on clear glass which became popular in the late medieval period (ffotograff).

Far right: This design for an architectural canopy is preserved on a mid-fourteenth-century glazing table used for the production of the windows of Girona Cathedral in Spain (Institut d'Estudis Catalans, Barcelona).

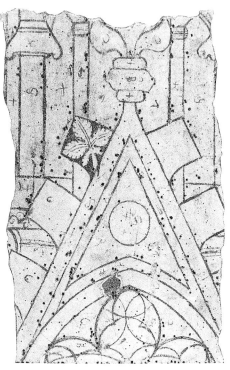

when paper became more common, the glaziers drew cartoons on paper, which could be reversed so that figures appeared in mirror image, and fewer had to be designed from scratch. Reversed images were particularly useful for attendant angels or prophets in series, but by now most figures in familiar biblical scenes had acquired standard poses, as can be seen in the Crucifixion with St John and the Virgin in the early sixteenth-century glass at the church of St Mary, Cilcain.

All the shapes that the glaziers needed were marked on the design, and the glass was cut to these shapes with a hot iron. The glaziers painted on such details as facial features and drapery folds. Over the years they developed subtle ways of shading and modelling, with elaborate stippling, which survives to great effect at Gresford.

The painted pieces were then fired in a kiln before being returned to the table to be joined together with lead. The ornamental effects produced by leading are an important aspect of the overall aesthetics of stained glass, as is the design of the iron armatures made by the blacksmith to support the glass in its final position. Restorations have often obscured this aspect, but you can get an idea of it from the great window showing the Tree of Jesse in the Denbighshire church of St Dyfnog, Llanrhaeadr-yng-Nghinmeirch.

This Tree of Jesse dates from 1533, just before the Reformation that burst upon the unsuspecting faithful and helped to destroy so much of the craftsmanship that this book celebrates.

By the late Middle Ages, the poses of figures in scenes like this early sixteenth-century Crucifixion in the church of St Mary in Cilcain (Flintshire) had become so well established that glaziers could reuse their cartoons (ffotograff).

These early sixteenth-century quarries in the church of St Meugan, Llanrhudd (Denbighshire), are decorated with delightful oak sprigs in yellow stain.

Stained and Painted Glass

The spectacular window in the north aisle of St Dyfnog's Church, Llanrhaeadr-yng-Nghinmeirch (Denbighshire), is dated 1533 in the lower right-hand corner.

The subject is the Tree of Jesse, which shows the ancestry of Christ as prophesied by Isaiah (11: 1–3). It occupies all five lights of the window. As is common in sixteenth-century glass, the design of the picture partly ignores the vertical mullions of the window: Jesse lies in a battlemented grey stone enclosure, which occupies the width of three lights.

The 'tree' grows from Jesse's side, curling into branches. The ancestors of Christ are accompanied by prophets; each figure is inscribed with his name. Some of the figures have been drawn from the same cartoon, reversed to show them in mirror image. The tree culminates with the Virgin and Child at the centre.

The colours in this window are particularly beautiful. The background is light blue, the flowers are yellow with white stems. David, son of Jesse, is dressed in a red tunic and green stockings beneath a dull pink, ermine-lined cloak. He holds a golden harp, his symbol as Psalmist.

David's white belt is made of flashed glass that has been abraded, that is, rubbed with emery to vary the shading. Another innovatory technique here is the use of red enamel to shade lips. The paint over the entire window has been stippled and variously shaded to give depth and movement to the figures.

Craftspeople in Wales Today

Wales's rich stock of surviving medieval buildings provides an enduring reminder of the labours of the builders and decorators described in this book. An equally important legacy of those craftsmen is the continuing use of their skills in the conservation and repair work carried out on the very buildings that they constructed.

Much, of course, has changed since the Middle Ages. New materials have been introduced, particularly during the last two centuries, and new techniques have developed alongside. Building can now take place all year round and modern machinery and methods have made tasks easier and safer. Yet, if we look at current practitioners of the trades described in this book we find that the skills are still largely the same. Fully trained masons, carpenters or stained-glass workers would not find it too difficult to fit in with their medieval counterparts.

However, fully trained craftspeople — who have mastered both modern and traditional techniques — are today in short supply. This is due, in part, to great changes in the building industry that occurred in the twentieth century. Many craftsmen died in the two world wars and so were unable to pass on their skills. Under urgent pressure to rebuild in Britain after 1945, new materials and methods were widely introduced. For instance, Portland Cement, which was patented as long ago as 1824, largely supplanted lime both in general construction and in the conservation of historic buildings in the wake of the Second World War. This has caused much damage to fragile structures, because cement is fundamentally incompatible with earlier materials. As a result, a 'lime revival' has been gathering pace during the last three decades. Such organizations as Cadw and the National Trust, which are responsible for the preservation of many sites, as well as private owners have become well aware of the dangers of applying inappropriate methods and materials to the historic structures in their care.

At the same time, there has been a general realization that craftspeople trained in the skills of their forebears and with a thorough knowledge of the benefits and limitations of traditional materials are crucial for the continuing preservation of our built heritage. In recent years, new training programmes and initiatives have been developed to try to attract suitable people to careers in building conservation.

Cadw sites across Wales provide excellent examples of the use of traditional methods in the conservation of historic buildings. At Tintern Abbey, craftspeople from Cadw have replaced decayed stonework with new dressed stones cut to the original profiles using medieval techniques. Their workshop looks very different from a medieval masons' lodge — brightly lit, furnished with power tools and equipped with dust extractors — but mouldings are still set out with templates and finished with a mason's hammer and chisels.

Opposite: The Cadw workshop at Tintern Abbey, where modern masons still employ the methods of medieval craftsmen. In the foreground, a mason has almost finished dressing a window mullion that had been set out with the template to the left.

The east wing of St Davids Bishop's Palace, where lime render has been used to protect vulnerable areas of stonework. Lime has been used throughout the recent conservation works at the site and vaults have been rebuilt using medieval techniques.

The bishop's palace at Llanddew (Breconshire) is a good example of a building conserved by a private individual using traditional methods and materials.

The senior carpenter at St Fagans National History Museum, near Cardiff, checks the fit of a mortice-and-tenon joint for a roof truss, just as a medieval craftsman would have done (National Museum of Wales).

At St Davids Bishop's Palace, recent conservation has included the rebuilding of vaults using medieval techniques and the use of lime for mortar and plaster in all procedures.

But high standards of conservation are not exclusive to Cadw and similar organizations. Communities and individuals have employed highly skilled craftspeople to carry out the sympathetic conservation and repair of churches, civic buildings, houses and other historic structures throughout Wales. St Cadoc's Church at Llangattock Lingoed (Monmouthshire) once again boasts a protective coat of lime render after conservation stabilized the structure and brought an important programme of wall paintings to light. An enthusiastic private owner oversaw the careful clearance and stabilization of a substantial portion of the ruined bishop's palace at Llanddew in Breconshire following the best principles of current conservation.

Just as in the Middle Ages, building with traditional materials and methods cannot be rushed. Unlike cement, lime mortar takes time to harden. Power tools may help craftspeople prepare materials more quickly, but the final dressing of mouldings or the cutting of timber joints still relies on the masterly and patient use of tools that are little different from those depicted in medieval manuscript illustrations. But time invested in the responsible conservation of historic buildings will ultimately pay dividends. Not only will costly repairs be unnecessary, but the built heritage of Wales will be preserved for future generations to enjoy.

Further information

For training in traditional building skills, visit the website of the National Heritage Training Group on: **www.nhtg.org.uk**

For conservation and maintenance of historic buildings, visit the website of the Society for the Preservation of Ancient Buildings on: **www.spab.org.uk**

For conservation and grant aid, visit Cadw's website on: **www.cadw.wales.gov.uk**

Forced to flee their respective countries when Europe was ravaged by war, Prince Juan Carlos and Princess Sofia fell in love on the magical island of Corfu. Fourteen years later, in the Royal Palace of Madrid, with Sofia at his side, Juan Carlos was formally declared King of Spain — the first new Spanish monarch for nearly three-quarters of a century. Together, they have helped change the face of Spain, guiding it out of the shadows of tyranny towards its rightful place in the sun.

Agencia Efe

Hola/Europa Press

HEIRS IN EXILE

BORN ON OPPOSITE SIDES OF EUROPE, A SPANISH PRINCE AND A GREEK PRINCESS WERE CONDEMNED TO CHILDHOOD EXILE – BEFORE THEY EVEN MET

♛ *As Spain was thrown into turmoil by civil war, a second child was born to Don Juan Carlos and Maria Mercedes* below. *From Rome, where the infant Prince Juan Carlos was born, the family continued to seek refuge from the unrest at home, first in Switzerland and later in Portugal. The Spanish heir apparent is shown* below right *aged six with his sister Pilar outside their home in Lausanne*

JUAN CARLOS VICTOR MARIA DE BORBON Y Borbon was born at 1.05 pm on 5 January 1938. His parents, Don Juan de Borbon y Battenberg, and Donna Mercedes de Borbon y Orleans, came from the Spanish and French lines of the Bourbon dynasty, respectively. His grandmother, Victoria Eugenie of Battenberg, was the granddaughter of Queen Victoria of England, and his grandfather was Alfonso XIII, the last King of Spain.

Juan Carlos's noble parentage meant that he was directly in line to the Spanish throne. Yet he had no constitutional rights as King, nor a country to rule over, for the once-noble Spanish monarchy was in exile. In April 1931, Alfonso, faced with increasing attempts by the people to overthrow him, had left Spain and fled into exile in France – an exile reinforced a few months later by the proclamation of the Second Republic, which took away his rights of Spanish citizenship and property.

Born in Rome

After travelling around Europe with his family, the tired and disillusioned King had finally settled in Rome. He lived in the constant hope that one day his people would feel the need to call him back. But the call did not come. In 1936, General Francisco Franco's nationalist forces had overthrown the Republic and plunged Spain into a bloody civil war that would leave its mark for ever. Now, two years later, the war was still continuing.

It was in these circumstances that Juan Carlos was born, at the Anglo American Hospital in Rome, to the great delight of his parents.

Popperfoto

Agencia Efe

They already had a daughter, Pilar, born in Cannes, in 1936. Now, with the birth of their son, the Royal line of Spain seemed set to continue.

For the first time since the death of Ferdinand VII in 1833, the two separate lines of the Bourbon dynasty had been reunited.

The early years

Juan Carlos's first years were spent at 112, Viale Paroli, a first-floor apartment in Rome, where he lived with his parents and sister. Within the next three years, he was to have a new sister, Margarita, and a brother, Alfonso.

Even in these early years, Juan Carlos's life was affected by political considerations. In 1941, when he was just three, his grandfather Alfonso renounced his rights to the Spanish throne in favour of his son Don Juan. A few months later, he was dead. Henceforth, Don Juan would be referred to as the Count of Barcelona, and Juan Carlos was his direct heir.

But the future of the Spanish monarchy was increasingly uncertain. The Spanish Civil War had ended in 1939 with the establishment of General Franco as *Caudillo* (Head of State). In addition, this year had also seen the outbreak of World War 2 and Franco seemed set to support Hitler. By 1941, the Italian leader Benito Mussolini had formed an alliance with Hitler, and, fearing for his family's safety, Don Juan sought refuge in the neutral territory of Switzerland.

For the next five years, the Royal Family's new home would be in Lausanne, in a house called Les Rocaillers, by the shores of Lake Geneva. Here, the Count of Barcelona gave Juan Carlos his first lessons, with the help of a governess, Mercedes Solano. The young Prince would later attend the school at Rolle.

In 1946, when World War 2 had ended, Juan Carlos's family moved yet again – this time to Portugal. After staying in various houses and hotels, in 1949 they finally settled on Villa Giralda, a beautiful house in Estoril, an attractive rural suburb of Lisbon. Now, at last, Juan Carlos could enjoy what was to be the happiest period of his youth.

A Greek childhood

On 2 November 1938, the same year as Juan Carlos's birth, Princess Sofia was born in Athens to Princess Federika of the House of Hanover – granddaughter of Kaiser Wilhelm – and Crown Prince Paul of Schleswig-Holstein, Heir Presumptive of his brother King George II of the Hellenes.

Her first home was in the Palace of Psychico, a modest but pleasant house in a residential area of Athens. In June 1940, her brother Constantine was born, and, despite the outbreak of World War 2, the Crown Prince and Princess of Greece's happiness seemed complete.

But their period of contentment was to be short-lived. In 1941, family tranquillity was shattered by the German invasion of Greece. As the Nazis neared Athens, it became clear that within a matter of days the capital would fall, and Federika, Sofia and Constantine left Athens for exile, boarding a hydroplane for Crete. But the bombings followed them, and they soon left the island on a British warship bound for Alexandria, where they were joined by Paul, his brother, King George, and sister, Princess Catherine.

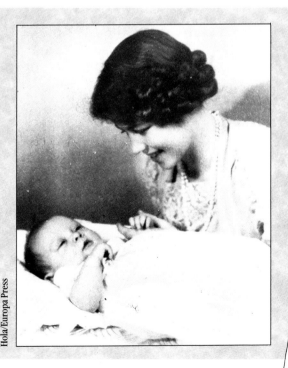

⚜ *Ten months after the birth of Juan Carlos, a first child was born to Crown Prince Paul and Princess Federika of Greece. As Federika gazed proudly at baby Sofia* below left, *the family were happily settled in the Royal Palace at Athens. Within three years, however, the family would be forced to flee as the Nazis advanced on the city. Prince Paul would spend the war years in Cairo, and Sofia would accompany her mother to South Africa, where they would remain until the war was over. Paul, with Federika at his side* below, *became King of Greece in 1946*

Hola/Europa Press

Popperfoto

👑 *In the summer of 1946, the Royal Family returned to Greece and settled in the Royal house at Psychico, eight miles from Athens. The King and Queen are* *shown standing in the garden outside the house, one year later. Princess Sofia and baby Irene are on the swing and Crown Prince Constantine rides his bicycle*

Popperfoto

The odyssey of Sofia and her family was to continue for several more years. Indeed, their real flight into exile had only just begun. From Alexandria, her mother boarded ship for Capetown in South Africa, with Constantine in her arms, Sofia by the hand, and Catherine at her side. Prince Paul and his brother, meanwhile, left for London. Paul himself would later return to Cairo.

Residence in South Africa

In Capetown, the South African Prime Minister, General (later Field Marshal) Smuts, took the family under his wing and they took up residence in Government House.

During these years, Federika wrote to her husband daily about the children's progress and, whenever she could, would leave the children in Princess Catherine's capable hands in order to visit him in Cairo. In April 1942, Federika gave birth to her third and last child, another daughter, in the small South African town of Irene, meaning 'peace'. The child – Irene – was christened there and then.

Shortly after Irene's birth, the family moved yet again – this time to Field Marshal Smuts's Pretoria residence. At times, it must have seemed as if the war would never end, and they would be condemned to perpetual exile. In 1944, the family stopped, briefly, in Cairo, soon moving on to Alexandria, where they stayed in the British Resident's house for two years. The children began to attend a local English day nursery, where Sofia would begin to add yet another language to her repertoire of Greek and German.

Finally, the war ended, and in 1946, the whole family returned to a Greece now torn by civil war. During their six years of exile, they had lived in no less than 22 homes.

The family decided to take up residence in their former holiday home, the Palace of Tatoi, nine miles from Athens. The house had been

THE PALACE OF TATOI

The Palace of Tatoi – former holiday home of the Greek Royal Family – became their permanent residence from 1946 onwards. An attractive, honey-coloured stone house, it was mainly decorated in the old English style, with wallpaper depicting English country life and hunting scenes, but furnished with French antiques. Its many other attractions included large, beautifully kept grounds, a marble swimming pool, and a specially constructed Cinemascope screen in the basement – all enough to keep the children entertained for hours

Rex Features

badly bombed during the war and had to be virtually rebuilt, but at last the family were able to move in. However, just five months after their return, King George of Greece died. Sofia's father Paul was now King, and she herself was heir to the Greek throne.

A haven of contentment

Juan Carlos would remember the years in Portugal as among the happiest of his life. The warm, sunny weather was a pure joy after the cold, wintry days of Switzerland, and the children took to their new outdoor life with great relish. Under the firm but loving guidance of their parents, days were spent swimming, sunbathing, and cycling – and there was always football if they really felt energetic.

These years were the closest approximation to 'normal' family life for Juan Carlos and his sisters and brothers: Pilar, elder sister and mentor to them all, the gentle Margarita – who, sadly, was blind – and, the favourite of all, Alfonso, his accomplice and occasional rival.

Much as they enjoyed Portugal, however, Spain was ever-present in their minds. Their home life was very much in the Spanish style, and traditions were reinforced by the fact that there was a considerable Spanish population where they lived.

Juan Carlos's education during these years was primarily in the hands of his tutor, Eugenio Vegas Latapie, who had been entrusted by Don Juan to make of his son 'a true Christian and Prince of Spain'. When it was decided, at the end of 1946, that Juan Carlos should attend the Ville St Jean, a boarding school run by the Marianist Fathers at Freiburg, Latapie went with him.

Working hard

Life at Freiburg was strict and disciplined, and the young Prince had to work hard at his studies. From a very early age, Juan Carlos had proved remarkably adept at languages. Now, by the age of six, he had already mastered French, English and, of course, Spanish, so these subjects came easily to him. He also quickly showed a great love for reading, matched only by a huge distaste for mathematics.

Juan Carlos's open, friendly manner and aptitude for sport soon made him popular. Nevertheless, the years at Freiburg were not happy ones. This was the first time the young Prince had been separated from his parents and he desperately missed the warmth and happiness of his home, which contrasted so deeply with the austerity of the school.

In the summer of 1948, a decision was taken that would affect Juan Carlos's entire future, and that of Spain. After years of silence, the Spanish Head of State, General Franco, sum-

Topham   Popperfoto

Topham

THE FORMATIVE YEARS

By the time he was 12, Juan Carlos led as 'normal' an existence as was possible for an heir to the throne. His life was divided between holidays in Portugal – he is shown *top* relaxing in the sea in Estoril – and school life in Spain. Lessons were strict – he is pictured *centre* during a geography lesson at the San Isidro Institute in Madrid with his tutor – but his competitive instinct was nurtured early. *Above* 'on his marks' – Juan Carlos prepares for a 100-metre dash at the same school

moned Juan Carlos's father, Don Juan, aboard his yacht, the *Azor*, in the Bay of Biscay. The subject under discussion was the future education of Juan Carlos, and Franco expressed his wish that Juan Carlos be educated in Spain.

As Don Juan agreed to give the matter his due attention, he must have pondered what Franco's motives for this request could have been. In any event, within a few months he had made his decision. On 8 September 1948, Juan Carlos and Alfonso boarded the Lusitania express train for Spain. The next day the Royal party arrived in Toledo. Juan Carlos was now ten years old. After a childhood spent in exile, he was at last in Spain.

Adolescence and first meeting

Sofia's early education took place against the background of a civil war that would end in 1951. For four years, she, her brother and sister attended a small private school at Psychico, with classes of ten children each, founded by Dr Jocelin Winthrop-Young. Non-school days were spent playing in the gardens of Tatoi.

In 1951, the Princesses Sofia and Irene were sent to Dr Kurt Hahn's boarding school at Schloss Salem in Baden-Wurttenberg, Germany – the very same school that their mother's cousin, the Duke of Edinburgh, had attended as a young boy in the 1930s.

Meanwhile, in Spain, Juan Carlos had begun to settle into his new home, Las Jarillas – a country mansion belonging to the Marquis and Marchioness of Urquijo that was about a dozen miles to the north of Madrid. The house was surrounded by woods and fields where Juan Carlos could indulge in his favourite sport of riding, in the company of his brother, Don Alfonso, when not studying at the San Isidro Institute in Madrid. Life continued in this vein, with the brothers spending most of the time in Spain, and their holidays in Portugal, where their sisters would anxiously await their return.

From 1950 onwards, they were to be based at the Palace of Miramar in San Sebastian. Discipline was strict, but at least they had the sea, and could continue their sporting interests. In 1954, Juan Carlos sat his final Baccalauréat examinations in Madrid, which he passed with flying colours. He was now 16, and free – for a few months at least – from the rigours of school.

With the passing of years, Sofia had grown up to be an attractive, polite and lively young woman, and was beginning to receive attention from boys of her age. By the summer of 1954, she, too, had finished her school term, and had just one more year's schooling to go. Her mother, Queen Federika, decided to arrange a cruise on her yacht, the *Agamemnon,* to which she would invite the sons and daughters of European Royalty. Juan Carlos was invited and, with his parents and elder sister, Pilar, boarded the yacht at Naples, bidding farewell to a tearful Margarita and Alfonso – they were considered too young to go. For a few glorious weeks, he and Sofia toured around the Greek islands in the company of young fellow Royals.

This, their first meeting, went totally unremarked upon. The two adolescents had not, it appeared, made much of an impression on one another, and when they returned to their respective homes at the end of the summer, nothing seemed to have changed. They did not know then that one day their lives would become inextricably linked.

> ## '*It is of the utmost importance that he is educated in Spain*'
>
> GENERAL FRANCO

♛ *As the young Prince and Princess approached maturity – he in Madrid, she in Athens – both began to discover the attractions of the opposite sex. Sofia is pictured* right *at her first ball in Corfu, where the Greek Royal Family had their summer residence, dancing with her brother and chaperone, Constantine, the heir apparent to the Greek throne. At the same time, Spain's most eligible bachelor* far right *was being introduced to admiring female guests at a gala ball given in his honour. He was to meet Sofia for the first time – albeit unmemorably – in the summer of 1954*

Europa Press

VILLA GIRALDA

Villa Giralda – a beautiful three-storeyed house in Estoril – was Juan Carlos's idyllic childhood home from the age of seven. The house itself – at 19 rua de Inglaterra – originally belonged to the Estoril golf club and was first leased by Don Juan. Although located in Portugal, Villa Giralda housed many mementoes from Spain, and as such provided a constant reminder of the young Prince's heritage

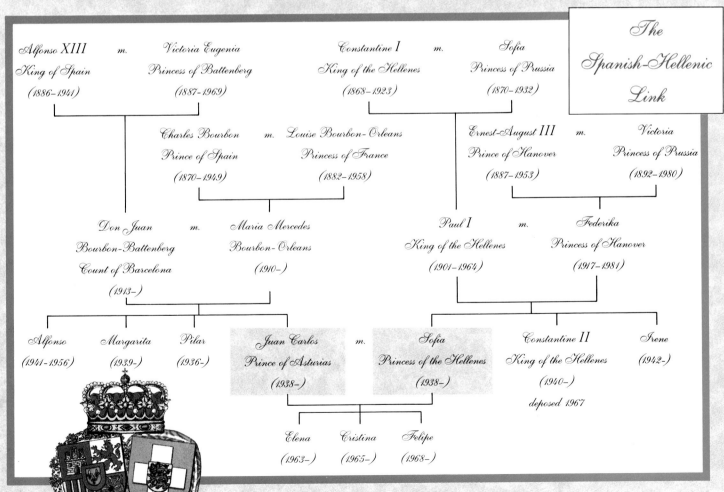

The
Spanish-Hellenic
Link

Alfonso XIII   m.   Victoria Eugenia
King of Spain   Princess of Battenberg
(1886–1941)   (1887–1969)

Constantine I   m.   Sofia
King of the Hellenes   Princess of Prussia
(1868–1923)   (1870–1932)

Charles Bourbon   m.   Louise Bourbon-Orleans
Prince of Spain   Princess of France
(1870–1949)   (1882–1958)

Ernest-August III   m.   Victoria
Prince of Hanover   Princess of Prussia
(1887–1953)   (1892–1980)

Don Juan   m.   Maria Mercedes
Bourbon-Battenberg   Bourbon-Orleans
Count of Barcelona   (1910–)
(1913–)

Paul I   m.   Federika
King of the Hellenes   Princess of Hanover
(1901–1964)   (1917–1981)

Alfonso   Margarita   Pilar
(1941–1956)   (1939–)   (1936–)

Juan Carlos   m.   Sofia
Prince of Asturias   Princess of the Hellenes
(1938–)   (1938–)

Constantine II   Irene
King of the Hellenes   (1942–)
(1940–)
deposed 1967

Elena   Cristina   Felipe
(1963–)   (1965–)   (1968–)

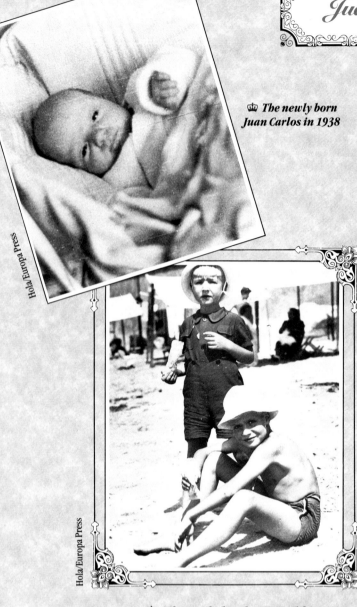

Hola/Europa Press

♕ *The newly born Juan Carlos in 1938*

Hola/Europa Press

♕ *A day on the beach at Estoril for Juan Carlos (seated) and Alfonso in 1946*

Agencia Efe

♕ *Maria Mercedes with, clockwise, Alfonso, Juan Carlos (aged nine), Pilar and Margarita*

Hola/Europa Press

♕ *The exiled King Alfonso XIII with his two young grandsons*

Topham

♕ *Back in Madrid. The Prince, aged 12, vaults over a friend*

♛ *Child-loving Sofia became godmother to her private tutor's daughter when she was 14*

♛ *Constantine, Sofia (aged eight) and Irene in national costume*

♛ *Sofia looks solemn at Constantine's christening in 1940*

♛ *Six-year-old Sofia working hard at her day nursery in Alexandria*

♛ *Sofia (front) and family at the 1947 anniversary celebration of Greece's entry into World War 2*

THE BOURBON HERITAGE

Nothing is more mysterious than the fate of the crown jewels of Spain, which were hidden by King Charles IV when his country was invaded by Napoleon Bonaparte in 1808, and never recovered – the crown shown here is purely symbolic. However, the Royal coat of arms remains as a colourful evocation of Spain's dramatic past

Europa Press

♛ The thrones used by Juan Carlos and Sofia are 18th-century-style reproductions of that used by King Charles III. They stand in the Throne Room of the Oriente Palace, under a magnificent canopy

Europa Press

Europa Press

♛ When Juan Carlos became King of Spain in 1975 there was no actual coronation – this symbolic crown used in the ceremony is of gilded silver, decorated with the emblems of the regions of Spain

The Royal coat of arms, seen here at the Oriente Palace, depicts the symbols of the ancient Spanish kingdoms. *Clockwise from top left* Castile, Leon, Navarre and Aragon, with the pomegranate of Granada at the bottom. It is surrounded by the chain of the Golden Fleece

 In this portrait, Juan Carlos wears the emblem of the famous chivalric order of the Golden Fleece. There are two branches of this Order, one Spanish and one Austrian. This split was decided in 1748, to settle a dispute between the Habsburgs and Bourbons

Europa Press

Europa Press

 The sceptre, like the crown, dates from the 19th century. It is of gold, covered in silver filigree and topped with a brilliant rock crystal

Rex Features

YOUNG LOVE

Camera Press

AS JUAN CARLOS STUDIED IN MADRID, SOFIA WIDENED HER HORIZONS IN ATHENS. IN 1961, APPROPRIATELY AT A ROYAL WEDDING, THEY NOTICED EACH OTHER FOR THE FIRST TIME

♔ *By now, Sofia was ready to embark on a short university career. She was already being tentatively courted by Prince Harald of Norway as she posed for this formal family portrait in the drawing-room of the Royal Palace at Athens. From left to right are Queen Federika, Sofia, King Paul, Irene and Crown Prince Constantine*

N 1954, JUAN CARLOS RETURNED TO ESTORIL. Once more, however, he was not destined to remain there for long. Towards the end of the year, his father and General Franco met and finally decided upon the future course of the Prince's education. In an Official Bulletin issued from the General's residence, El Pardo, it was announced that he would 'continue his studies and complete his education in Spain, for better service to the Fatherland and in consequence of his position in the dynastic line'.

In January 1955, Juan Carlos moved to Madrid and began his studies at the small palace of Montellano where, under the supervision of General Martinez Santos, the Duke of La Torre, he prepared for the entrance examination to the General Military Academy at Saragossa. The Duke imposed a rigorous timetable upon the young Prince – a 12-hour day from 8 am to 8 pm that included lessons in mathematics (including geometry and trigonometry), English and military studies. This was a stern introduction to royal responsibilities, especially to a youth whose future role in Spain must have seemed as uncertain as the days of exile he had already endured.

A military training

His efforts were rewarded, however, and just before Christmas he entered the Military Academy as a cadet, taking his oath of allegiance on 15 December. After the ceremony, Juan Carlos immediately sent off a telegram to his father in Estoril. 'Before the flag of Spain I have promised to be a perfect soldier. With great emotion I swear to you that I will fulfil my promise.' But barracks life was not easy for him, especially as a young prince. Consequently, Juan Carlos was quick to set about reducing the distance between himself and the other 269 cadets who had enlisted alongside him. He had been there no time at all before his fellow cadets humorously began referring to him as 'Sar' (SAR – *Su Alteza Real*; His Royal Highness). As one of his companions put it, 'Sar' would be put through all the harshest aspects of military training 'just like the rest of us'.

Student and nurse

But just as the young Prince was being toughened up by the discipline of the parade ground, Sofia, her years at Salem ended, returned to the Palace of Tatoi. By now she was

Rex Features

17 and, once back in Athens, was determined to have a say in her own future.

Sofia's interest in the classics and archaeology had always been strong, and for a while she returned to university to pursue these subjects. Ever-interested in music, she also joined a local amateur choir that frequently performed with visiting professional orchestras. Unlike Juan Carlos, there were no political pressures on Sofia, and she was free to pursue many other interests during these years, such as photography, drawing and sports – especially sailing, an interest she shared with her brother Constantine. Her proficiency in this sport was so great, in fact, that she was later chosen as a reserve in the 1960 Olympic Games.

Within little more than a year, however, she had enrolled for a two-year-long course at the Mitera Institute of Paediatric Nursing, and later practised at a foundling hospital in Athens. Although she was to continue her interests in music, archaeology and the classics, Sofia felt that by nursing she was placing herself closer to her people – a consideration she would later regard as important when Queen of Spain.

An untimely death

During the Holy Week of 1956, Juan Carlos returned to Estoril for the holidays. As ever, he was thoroughly happy to be back within the family fold. However, on the Thursday evening of that week, tragedy struck: Juan, Margarita and Alfonso were passing the time before dinner. The two young men were talking together while Alfonso was cleaning a pistol which had recently been received as a present. Juan Carlos had just turned round for a second when a hollow explosion rang out in the room. He quickly turned – just in time to see his younger brother fall to the ground, fatally wounded. While Juan Carlos held the unconscious Alfonso in his arms, Margarita ran to find their parents. Don Juan arrived and attempted to stem the flow of blood, but Alfonso was not to regain consciousness. The legendary bad luck of the Bourbons had returned. Twenty-two years before, in Austria, Alfonso XIII's youngest son had died in Don Juan's arms as a result of a similar shooting accident.

Alfonso's death was heartbreaking for Juan Carlos. Many years later, he wrote a moving epitaph to his brother: 'Alfonso was always restless and bright. He was of exceptional intelligence, with an incredible ability for noticing things which would pass by the attention of others. Furthermore he was one to speak his mind openly, and without going the long way about it. He would make us all laugh . . .'

Alfonso was laid to rest in Portugal under Spanish soil specially transported from Extre-

Robert Hunt Library

madura. He was buried with his body wrapped in Spain's national flag.

Juan Carlos returned to the Military Academy after the funeral and by July 1957 he had attained the rank of Infantry Second Lieutenant. A month later, he reported to the Naval School in Marin as a midshipman, and by

♛ *Juan Carlos returned to Estoril for his parents' silver wedding anniversary above. From left to right are Margarita, Pilar, Don Juan, Maria Mercedes and Juan Carlos, but by this time there was no Alfonso*

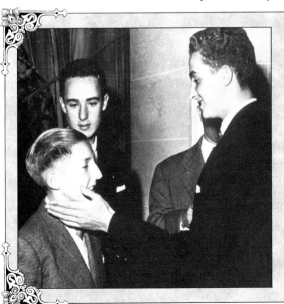

A FAMILY TRAGEDY

In 1956, during a holiday spent at Estoril, Juan Carlos's younger brother Alfonso *left* was fatally wounded in a freak shooting accident at the Villa Giralda. Juan Carlos had been particularly attached to his brother and he was deeply scarred by the tragic incident

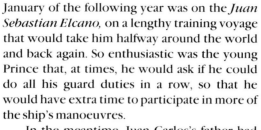

👑 *During a visit to America, Sofia took time to meet Greek orphans who had found new homes there. Her interest in children all over the world was to remain with her throughout her life*

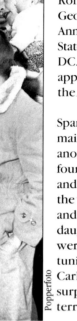

January of the following year was on the *Juan Sebastian Elcano,* on a lengthy training voyage that would take him halfway around the world and back again. So enthusiastic was the young Prince that, at times, he would ask if he could do all his guard duties in a row, so that he would have extra time to participate in more of the ship's manoeuvres.

In the meantime, Juan Carlos's father had caused a great stir by crossing the Atlantic in his yacht, the *Saltillo*, so that he could meet his son in America. Together, father and son went to visit George Washington's house, the Roman Catholic University of Georgetown, the Naval School of Annapolis and finally the United States Congress in Washington DC. The Prince's photograph appeared on the front page of the *New York Times*.

Although the Greek and Spanish Royal Families had maintained contact with one another, by 1958 it had been four years since Juan Carlos and Sofia had last met. It was at the wedding of one of the Duke and Duchess of Württemberg's daughters at Stuttgart that they were provided with the opportunity to meet again. That Juan Carlos arrived at all was surprising. Flying over French territory on his way to the

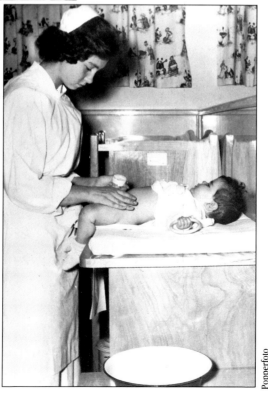

👑 *Sofia gave a great deal of her time to the welfare and care of children in her own country. At the age of 18, she started to train as a nurse at the Athens Home for Abandoned Children. She is shown right 'cleaning up' one of the babies*

wedding, the control tower at Bordeaux refused him permission to land for refuelling. Eventually, the plane was forced to make an emergency landing and Juan Carlos, in full naval dress uniform, was hurried to Althausen Castle to attend the reception.

This time, Juan Carlos and Sofia danced and chatted together. Some of the guests in attendance remarked that they made a nice couple, and indeed one of Juan Carlos's companions congratulated him on his good fortune. Juan replied: 'Ah yes, the Princess Sofia of Greece. She has cast me in her spell.'

In the summer of 1960, the Prince graduated with honours from the Military Academy. He had rounded off his training with the General Air Force Academy of St Javier in Murcia. This was enough to convince him that he preferred sailing to flying. Sofia, meanwhile, had finished her training in nursing, and two brief works by her on archaeology had been published to favourable reviews. During his training, Juan Carlos had made many practice flights to Italy, and in Naples the couple met again briefly, as they watched Sofia's brother Constantine win a gold medal for yachting at the Olympics.

The student Prince

Following his father's advice, Juan Carlos enrolled at Madrid University in spring 1960. Although the decision was his alone, there were those who sympathized with the arduous nature of his royal apprenticeship. His uncle, Don Alfonso de Orleans, said: 'They are going to make an expert out of him … In all my 70 years I have never seen such a complicated life as that which is being imposed on the Prince of Asturias.'

Life was more relaxed on the campus in Madrid than it had been with the military, however. Juan Carlos chose to study a number of subjects including political economy, Spanish history and literature, social and political law and philosophy. He began to accumulate a number of new ideas about his future role, some of which were not warmly received in government circles. General Franco himself observed the first hints that the Prince was sympathetic to democracy with distaste, and observed in his diary: 'A King for all Spaniards … I don't like the sound of that.' As events after 1975 were to prove, the old General never came to understand how strongly Juan Carlos was influenced by his years at university.

Juan Carlos had been at Madrid for just over a year when he received an invitation to the wedding, in England, of the Duke and Duchess of Kent's son Edward to Lady Katherine Worsley. The ceremony was to be held in York Minster on 8 June – the first Royal

A ROYAL APPRENTICESHIP

As the result of a meeting between General Franco and Don Juan, it was decided that it would stand Juan Carlos in good stead to undergo training with the Spanish Armed Forces; with Spain under military control, the General reckoned this to be an important stage in his successor's education. Starting in 1954 at the age of 17, the young Prince's military initiation lasted three and a half years, during which time he gained experience in each of the three Services.

By 1958 he had obtained commissions as an Infantry lieutenant, Naval sub-lieutenant and Air Force flying-officer and had travelled around much of the world. As a pilot, one of his many practice flights gave him the opportunity to meet Sofia in Naples, while as a midshipman he went on a training voyage that introduced him to many of the countries of the Americas, including Panama, Peru, Colombia, the Dominican Republic and finally the United States.

His enthusiasm as an officer was noticeable, as was the fact that he never expected to be treated any more indulgently than his fellow cadets. But, unlike his neighbouring European monarchs, his military role was to be far from ornamental; today he is the Supreme Commander of the Spanish Armed Forces

wedding to be held in here for over 600 years.

Princess Sofia, too, had received an invitation to the wedding – she would be going with her brother Constantine, who would act as chaperone. At the time she was having some problems dealing with the advances of Harald, the King of Norway's son, and it was felt that a brief journey could, perhaps, clear the air. Juan Carlos's name, too, had been linked elsewhere. It was rumoured that he would soon become engaged to his life-long companion, Princess Maria Gabriela of Savoy, daughter of King Umberto of Italy. But fate was to decree otherwise.

On the day of the wedding, a fortuitous coincidence occurred. The mysterious workings of protocol had laid down that Juan Carlos was to accompany Princess Sofia during the reception after the ceremony. That evening, the couple managed to get to know one another better in the space of a few hours than they had ever managed before. Many years afterwards, Queen Elizabeth herself would assert that 'it all began that night at the Duke of Kent's wedding.'

♛ *Shortly after he completed his military training, the young Prince was finally allowed the opportunity to relax. He is photographed left in the summer of 1959 strolling around St Tropez with a friend during his travels round the Mediterranean on his father's yacht* Saltillo

Topham

👑 **Above** *Juan Carlos teasingly cajoles his new fiancée to smile for the world's photographers at Lausanne in Switzerland shortly after the official announcement of their engagement*

👑 *The courtship had lasted three months from the time the couple met at York Minster in June. Up to the last moment, there had been worries that General Franco's consent to their marriage might not be forthcoming*

Zefa

Europa Press

AEGEAN INTERLUDE

By further coincidence, both Sofia and Juan Carlos were staying in the Savoy Hotel during their visit to England. On the day after the wedding, the Prince joined Sofia and her brother Constantine for tea. It was the beginning of what turned out to be a drawn-out summer courtship in London. Years later, Queen Sofia confessed: 'We were alone. We were without our parents, and we more or less got engaged in London.'

Both their respective parents and the European press became aware that there was more than met the eye to Sofia and Juan Carlos's dallying in London. Telephone calls between London and Spain and London and Greece gradually revealed that a Royal romance was blossoming and newspapers were full of speculation about the match-making roles of Victoria Eugenie and Federika. But this was not to be an arranged marriage. As Sofia was later to recall about their most decisive meeting: 'For once protocol got it right and assigned him as my escort, and that was that.'

Aegean holiday

The reaction from Estoril and Athens was one of enormous pleasure. The King and Queen of Greece immediately invited Prince Juan Carlos and his mother and father to spend a brief holiday in Corfu with them and their family. There was perhaps an element of scheming in Queen Federika's choice of holiday spot – an opportunity to strengthen the relationship between the couple – for in her opinion 'Corfu is the most beautiful place in the world to fall in love.'

They sailed around the waters of the island, blissfully happy, although years later, and with a twinkle in her eye, Sofia said: 'Once, when we were not engaged, I went on a yacht with Juan. The boat's crew always ended up arguing among themselves and after that I still cannot understand how I was ever able to marry him!'

However, it was another month before they announced their future plans to the world at large. Towards the end of the second week in September, they and their parents met at 'Vieille Fontaine', Victoria Eugenie's home in Lausanne. Don Juan and Maria de las Mercedes could not agree more with their son's choice of bride-to-be and finally, late one afternoon, Juan Carlos proposed to Sofia. Without any hesitation she accepted.

That same afternoon, Don Juan telephoned the palace of El Pardo in Madrid to inform General Franco. The line was so poor that the two of them could barely hear one another, but eventually Don Juan deciphered Franco's reply

– 'Enhorabuena' (congratulations). Looking around her with pride, Federika exclaimed: 'Sofia will make a perfect Queen of Spain!'

Her new fiancé was no less full of optimism. In an interview given to the Spanish magazine, *La Actualidad Española*, Juan Carlos expressed his deep admiration for Sofia: 'Her greatest quality is her deep sense of duty. She's cheerful, charming, totally unaffected and kind. She is home-loving and adores children. I'm sure the Spanish people will love her.'

But before she could go to Spain as Juan Carlos's wife there were many arrangements to make. The great day had been set for 14 May 1962. It would be a spring wedding.

♛ *From Switzerland the couple went to Athens to be fêted by the Greek people on their engagement. Along with other members of the Royal Family, they also took part in the Royal regatta there below*

Rex Features

THE PALACIO DE ORIENTE

In 1734, on Christmas Eve, Madrid's Royal palace, the old Moorish Alcázar, burned to the ground. Its dazzling replacement, the Oriente, was started in 1738 when King Philip V commissioned designs by the Italian architect, Filippo Juvarra. This work was continued by Juan Battista Sacchetti, but Philip V died before it was completed – 26 years later. Now Juan Carlos and Sofia prefer Zarzuela Palace, using the Oriente only for official functions

Image Bank

Quim Llenas/Cover

♔ The Oriente Palace *top* is a spectacular sight, with a façade that was inspired by that of the Louvre, in Paris. Juan Carlos and Sofia pose in formal dress for an official occasion at the Palace

♔ Madrid, 2000 feet above sea level, is the highest capital in Europe, so the wide patio of the Palace *left* has a glass roof to protect it from the elements

♔ The great Spanish artist, Francisco Goya, served as court painter in the 18th century. Some of his work is displayed in the Goya Room *right*, set off by white silk walls and Spanish Empire furniture

Rex Features

👑 King Alfonso XIII and Queen Victoria Eugenie, the grandparents of Juan Carlos, were the last Royal couple to live in the Oriente. Victoria Eugenie's bedroom *right*, with its lavish peach silk hangings and delicately painted bed, is kept exactly as she left it

👑 The magnificent Throne Room *below* is one of the most sumptuous rooms in the Palace. The lovely cloud blue ceiling was painted in 1764 by the Venetian artist G B Tiepolo, who spent the last years of his life in Madrid. The four gilded lions guarding the throne were saved from the Alcázar fire of 1734. The huge chandeliers are Venetian

Fernando Sacristan/Cover

Hola/Europa Press

Edistudio

Edistudio

Europa Press

♔ King Alfonso XIII's study *top left*, kept as it was during his lifetime, contrasts with the extravagance of the rest of the Palace. An intimate touch is provided by photographs of his Queen and their grandchildren

♔ One of the most beautiful and luxurious rooms in the Palace is the drawing-room *top right*, named after Mattia Gasparini, the Neapolitan painter who decorated the ceiling with flowers, fruit and birds in high relief

♔ Three rooms were combined in the 19th century by King Alfonso XII to produce the splendid banqueting hall *left*, where 145 guests can be seated. This room is used at Christmas by Juan Carlos and Sofia for a grand family dinner. The porcelain dates from the 18th century and over 100 lights illuminate the scene

John Frost

ATHENIAN WEDDING

THE SETTING FOR THE WEDDING COULD NOT HAVE BEEN BETTERED; THE HONEYMOON WAS THE STUFF THAT DREAMS ARE MADE OF – AND THE BIRTH OF A DAUGHTER SET THE SEAL ON JUAN CARLOS AND SOFIA'S HAPPINESS

👑 *On one of her last engagements before the wedding, Sofia captivated the inhabitants of a border village in northern Greece* inset, left, *but as the big day drew nearer she had eyes only for Juan Carlos. She is seen* left *buttoning up his jacket prior to a photocall. He was wearing his left arm in a sling after dislocating his shoulder during a bout of judo with Sofia's brother, Constantine*

👑 *Excitement grew as the wedding approached. Girls wearing traditional Greek costume showered the couple with flower petals when they attended an athletics meeting* below

THE EIGHT MONTHS BETWEEN THE ENGAGE-ment and wedding must have seemed like an eternity to Juan Carlos and Sofia. But certain matters of Church proto-col had to be arranged before the ceremony could take place. Sofia's family were members of the Greek Orthodox Church. Although Sofia herself had agreed to take the Catholic faith, she and her family wanted a Greek Orthodox ceremony to follow the Catholic wedding, and the permission of the Vatican had to be sought. Similar matters of protocol had been confronted – and resolved – when Alfonso XIII had married the Anglican Victoria Eugenie.

Before the year was out, Juan Carlos accompanied his father to seek a papal audience with Pope John XXIII at the Vatican. Their problems were listened to with great courtesy and understanding, and the Pontifical Brief, agreeing to both ceremonies and dis-pensing with any possible impediments to the marriage, duly arrived towards the end of the winter. Now, to everyone's relief, the wedding arrangements could begin.

The following Easter, Sofia accompanied her parents to the Villa Giralda in Estoril – her first-ever visit to Portugal. Here, while the families discussed the wedding arrangements, the two lovers spent idyllic days alone, walking on the beaches, their mutual feelings for each other growing with each passing day. But time passed all too quickly, and soon Sofia had to return to Greece. Although months of separation were inevitably to follow, the couple would be in constant contact, exchanging letters, flowers and phone calls at every opportunity.

Juan Carlos, meanwhile, boarded an aeroplane for Madrid where, as a matter of courtesy, he visited the Head of State, General Franco. The 'Generalissimo' would not be able to attend the wedding, but he gave the couple his blessing and his very best wishes for the future.

Wedding of the decade

By now, the wedding arrangements were in full swing, and it seemed that the event might prove the Royal wedding of the decade. Juan Carlos was to receive the Order of Charles III; there was no higher compliment that the Spanish State could confer on the Prince. From the Greek Government he received the Plaque of the Holy Greek Cross of Christ the Redeemer.

The vast guest list, which included dignitaries and Royalty from all over the world, had been drawn up and the invitations sent off. From the earliest days of spring, wedding presents for the couple had been arriving from all four corners of the globe. Gifts for Sofia included a large, diamond-studded brooch from the Ministry of Naval Affairs, a crocodile-skin vanity case from President de Gaulle, and a sable fur coat from Aristotle Onassis. Other

Popperfoto

Popperfoto

AGE Fotostock

presents for the couple included an ornamental solid gold oil tanker from the Greek multi-millionaire Stavros Niarchos, a gold cigarette case from American President John Kennedy, a Persian carpet from the Shah of Iran, a sporting yacht from Prince Rainier and Princess Grace of Monaco, a solid silver dinner service from Queen Elizabeth and Prince Philip – and a writing desk from General Franco.

Meanwhile, many Spaniards were making their own private preparations. Several liners had been privately chartered to make the trip from Spain to Greece. And, not to be outdone, the Italians arranged for several more ships to set sail from Brindisi when the great day drew nearer.

The amount of well-wishing was indeed phenomenal. A small group of the Spanish faithful, in league with certain more adventurous editorial entrepreneurs, decided to launch a Spanish newspaper in Athens – the *Athens Spanish Daily* – during the week of festivities surrounding the wedding. Donations to help produce the paper were received into a bank account in Athens, and funds raised were to go (in Princess Sofia's name) to the aid of mothers in need.

A family reunion

The last few weeks of festivities were frenzied, as thousands of Spanish patriots flooded into the Greek capital. In mid-April, Don Juan boarded his yacht, the *Saltillo,* which was lying at anchor in the port of Lisbon, and set sail for the Greek mainland. When he arrived at the harbour of Piraeus almost a week later, on 22 April, his son and future daughter-in-law were standing on the quayside to greet him.

As Don Juan took his first steps on to the quayside, Sofia immediately moved forward to embrace him, while her husband to be – enormously moved by her simple devotion – remained slightly to one side. Then, in a tender and thoughtful gesture, Sofia embraced her

Popperfoto

Topham

future father-in-law and, resting her right hand on his shoulder, stretched her head forward for Don Juan to trace the sign of the cross on her brow. The most sacred and aged of Bourbon family traditions had thus been honoured.

Two weeks later, as the first issue of the *Athens Spanish Daily* came on to the news-stands, the first ships began to arrive from Barcelona, Alicante, Cadiz (and, of course, Brindisi). As the 'floating hotels' lay anchored at Piraeus, music and far-off laughter came wafting over on the evening breeze to echo around the harbour walls. The winding streets were festooned with bunting – blue and white, for Greece, and red and yellow, for Spain.

Countdown to the ceremony

On the morning of Friday 11 May, with less than three days to go before taking their marriage vows, Juan Carlos and Sofia attended a reception given by the Mayor of Athens – the first to be given in their honour. That night a gala reception was given for them in the Throne Room at the Royal Palace. So many people had wanted to come that there was not enough room to hold them, and instead of one reception there were several – each attended by Juan Carlos and Sofia, who greeted their guests personally.

The next day the Greek Royal Family held a grand reception in the gardens of the Palace of Tatoi for the many Spanish guests that had arrived in the capital. Of all the thousands of people who attended, the silver-haired Queen Victoria Eugenie was truly the star of the occasion.

By Sunday 13 May – the eve of the wedding – excitement had reached fever pitch. The exact nature of Sofia's wedding gown was still being kept a tight secret, but word was out that the Paris fashion designer, Greek-born Jean Dessès, was the man to whom any further enquiries were to be directed. As the lights went out that night, Sofia and Juan Carlos, both

RED LETTER DAY

For the crowds who lined the wedding route, craning from windows and rooftops, it was a day to remember. The first marriage ceremony – attended by 137 members of foreign Royalty, as well as statesmen from all over the world – was completed by the exchange of rings *inset*, whereupon Juan Carlos and Sofia became husband and wife. The happy couple received a military send-off when they emerged from the Roman Catholic Cathedral into bright sunlight *below* and rode back to the Royal Palace in the ceremonial coach

Popperfoto

Rex Features

beaming with excitement, arrived at Piraeus just in time for a gigantic fireworks display, watched by thousands.

Wedding day

As Monday 14 May dawned, a coach and six white horses awaited Sofia in the courtyard of the Royal Palace. A dun-coloured stallion stood tethered by their side. Shortly after 9 am, Sofia was helped into the coach by her father, King Paul, while her brother Constantine, dressed in Hussar's uniform, mounted the brown horse. After a bugle blast, wheels ground on cobbled stones as the procession, preceded by open-topped cars bearing Sofia's parents, began its one-mile journey to the Cathedral of St Dionysius, where the Catholic ceremony was to take place. The massive crowds cheered and bands played as the carriage made its way along the streets. In Venicelos Street, immediately before the Cathedral, the band of a Spanish cruiser struck up the Spanish National Anthem. It was followed, after a brief pause, by that of Greece.

The Cathedral was bedecked with 40,000 red and yellow carnations, representing the colours of Spain. Holding a sprig of lily of the valley in her pale, ungloved hand, Sofia mounted the first of the steps leading to the entrance. As she entered the Cathedral, her embroidered train – six yards in length – was carried by eight Princesses: Pilar of Spain, Irene of Holland, Alexandra of Kent (Sofia's close childhood friend), Tatiana Radziwill, Benedicta and Anne-Marie of Denmark, Anne of France and Irene Eugenie of Greece. Father and daughter walked the length of the central aisle as the choir sang a chorus from Handel's *Messiah*, while Juan Carlos, wearing his khaki lieutenant's uniform, waited for his bride to join him at the altar rail.

Afterwards the couple posed briefly outside the entrance to the Cathedral. As Juan Carlos lowered his lips to kiss his bride's upturned face, the sky rained rose petals; cameras flashed and the onlookers roared.

The wedding breakfast

Then, descending the steps of the Cathedral in pairs, came the pride of world Royalty: King Olaf of Norway and Queen Juliana of Holland, Queen Victoria Eugenie of Spain and Queen Ingrid of Denmark, Queen Mother Elena of Romania and Prince Berhnhardt of Holland, King Umberto and Queen Maria Jose of Italy, the Sovereign Prince and Princess of Liechtenstein; Prince Rainier and Princess Grace of Monaco, the Prince of Luxemburg and Princess Josephine Carlota of Belgium … Back in the Royal Palace, Juan and Sofia enjoyed a brief

'BY INVITATION ONLY'

The wedding was the social highlight of the year and invitations were highly prized. At the wedding dinner, dominated by the spectacular cake *right*, each guest was presented with a silver box *below*, engraved with the Royal coats of arms of Greece and Spain, as a memento of a unique occasion. Afterwards, the glittering gathering happily posed for pictures on the steps of the Royal Palace

Europa Press

Hola/Europa

Europa Press

Topham

MEMO

LEG LAMB (6 lb) IN HAY
4 ozs Butter
HERBS - TYME OR "
COVER TIN WITH HAY
LAY LAMB Then cover
with Butter & Herbs
Then cover with HAY
Then cover all over
with Foil
Bake FOR 2½ hrs

FREE COLLECTION & DELIVERY!

wedding breakfast with their relations, friends and attendants. In less than an hour's time the Greek Orthodox ceremony would follow.

A second ceremony

As Juan Carlos and Sofia stepped together into the coach to make their way to the Greek Orthodox Cathedral for the second wedding ceremony, yet another half million Greeks and Spaniards lined the streets, and as they cheered all the bells of all the churches of the capital rang out.

According to tradition, at the end of the service the guests worked their way silently around the newlyweds in the ritual dance of Isaiah, in which rice and rose petals were flung on to the couple from outstretched hands. Queen Federika kissed the couple on their cheeks. Then she and Countess Maria watched in silence as their loved ones strolled forth from the church and into the bright afternoon sunlight.

By 5.30 in the evening, the time had come for farewells. Juan Carlos left his wife's side briefly, to return in a sports car that was parked ready and waiting. Some well-wishers had impaled a bright, unskinned orange on the front radio aerial, while tin cans trailed from the rear of the car.

As Queen Federika hugged her eldest daughter, emotions finally took over, and both women burst into tears. The family embraced, then Sofia climbed into the sports car to sit by her husband's side.

At the port of Torcolimanos, the yacht *Eros* lay waiting to take the couple to the small island of Spetsopoula in the Aegean – the first stage of their honeymoon. Shortly afterwards, Don Juan boarded his yacht, the *Saltillo*, to begin his voyage back to Estoril. The rest of the family were to follow a few days later.

> '*It was a glorious day. Sofia looked breathtakingly beautiful*'
>
> QUEEN FEDERIKA

♛ *Juan Carlos and Sofia enjoyed an idyllic Mediterranean honeymoon aboard the yacht* Eros, *a gift from their close friends Prince Rainier and Princess Grace of Monaco. They are seen* bottom *strolling in the Italian resort of Portofino, and* below *waving to well-wishers in the little harbour of Anzio*

Popperfoto

Hulton-Deutsch Collection

BIRTH OF THE INFANTA

By 20 May, after a week of sailing around the Greek islands, Juan Carlos and Sofia were back in Corfu, where, in a quiet ceremony in the presence of the Archbishop of Athens, Sofia officially entered the Roman Catholic Church. At the beginning of June, the couple started their return journey to Spain, stopping off in Rome for a few days to pay Pope John XXIII a courtesy visit of thanks for his help before the wedding. On 6 June, they landed at Getafe Airport near Madrid, to be hailed by the Head of State as the 'Prince and Princess of Spain'. But their stay in Spain was to be only the briefest of interludes in which to give thanks to the Spanish people. They were about to begin the second, and most important, phase of their honeymoon.

A few days after their return to Spain, Juan Carlos and Sofia embarked on a four-month-long trip around the world. The tour was organized privately by a travel agency, and the couple travelled incognito for most of the time. It was reported that 'not even a maid or policeman' was accompanying them.

The first stop was Monte Carlo, where they visited Prince Rainier and Princess Grace of Monaco – who had been guests at their wedding. Within a day of their arrival, a gala reception was held in their honour at Monte Carlo's famed Sporting Club – attended by such glittering show-business personalities as Robert Wagner, Yul Brynner and Frank Sinatra.

East and west

From Monte Carlo, the couple sailed to Portofino, in Italy. After a few days there and in Rome, they were to begin an extensive tour of the East. India, Nepal, Thailand, Hong Kong and Japan were all part of a glorious itinerary that Juan Carlos and Sofia would always remember.

Their favourite place, however, was the USA, where they stayed for a month, visiting San Francisco, Los Angeles (where they visited the MGM Studios in Hollywood) and New York. Some even claimed to have seen the couple sitting quietly at a restaurant on the corner of 49th Street and Fifth Avenue in New York City, eating beefburgers together.

Sadly, however, it was by now September and their tour had come to an end. On their way back, the couple passed through London, where Sofia commented to a newspaper reporter, 'I wish it could have lasted forever.'

No sooner had they returned, than tragedy

GOING PLACES

During their globe-trotting honeymoon trip, Juan Carlos and Sofia were fêted by monarchs and statesmen alike. In Monaco, they were Princess Grace's guests *above* for a cabaret evening starring Frank Sinatra. Later, President Kennedy welcomed them to the White House *inset*, and invited them on a tour of Cape Canaveral

struck Spain. At the end of September 1962, the province of Catalonia suffered terrible floods, resulting in death, devastation and, for many people, homelessness. At Sofia's insistence, the Royal couple immediately went to the scene of the disaster, where they attended the funerals of the victims and consoled families of the bereaved. The occasion provided Juan Carlos and Sofia's first personal contact with the Spanish people, who were instantly warmed by their obvious concern.

In March 1963, after six months of building work to convert it into a family residence, the Royal couple's new home was ready. It was to be in Spain itself, in the Palace of Zarzuela, just three miles to the north of Madrid. A relatively modest dwelling by royal standards, the Palace had originally been built as a hunting lodge in the later part of the 17th century – rather appropriately during the reign of Philip V, the first Bourbon King of Spain.

Like many other, perhaps more ordinary, couples, Juan Carlos and Sofia just wanted to settle down in peace and quiet, to build a home and a family. Before 1963 was over their wishes were to come true. Princess Sofia discovered she was pregnant.

Holy baptism

The Infanta Elena was born at 2pm on Friday 20 December 1963, at the Hospital of Our Lady of Loreto in Madrid. Three hours later, an overjoyed Juan Carlos, having telephoned his parents, celebrated the new arrival by drinking champagne with the waiting reporters.

Exactly one week later Elena was baptized in the Palace of Zarzuela by the Papal Nuncio, Monsignor Riberi, who performed the ceremony with holy water from the Jordan. The baptism was a momentous occasion, attended by General Franco and his wife Carmen Polo. Juan Carlos's father, Don Juan, was also present – it was his first visit to Madrid since his exile in 1931.

For Prince Juan Carlos and Princess Sofia, family life had now well and truly begun.

👑 *The newlyweds made their first home together at the Villa Giralda in Estoril in the autumn of 1962* top. *The following year they moved to Madrid and Sofia became pregnant – to the delight of Don Juan, pictured* above *greeting his daughter-in-law shortly before the birth. The baby was christened Elena Maria Isabel Dominica de Silos by her proud parents* right

Popperfoto

Hulton-Deutsch Collection

Diamond jewellery – a wedding present from Queen Frederika of Grece

LA REINA ELEGANTE

For her wedding, Princess Sofia followed the custom of our own Royal Family and chose her mother's favourite designer – Greek-born Jean Dessès. Since her marriage, she has favoured Spanish couturiers, notably Pertegaz and Elio Berhanyer, wearing their clothes with such style that she has become her country's best ambassadress of fashion. As a graceful gesture, she wears the traditional mantilla on some official occasions. She loves dramatic evening dresses and these are now sometimes borrowed by her daughters – surely the ultimate compliment!

♛ Sofia sparkled in this lovely ballgown, worn just before her wedding. It has an unusual petalled skirt

Rows of narrow silver lace

Popperfoto

♛ The bridegroom wore the pale blue sash of the Order of Charles III over his army uniform

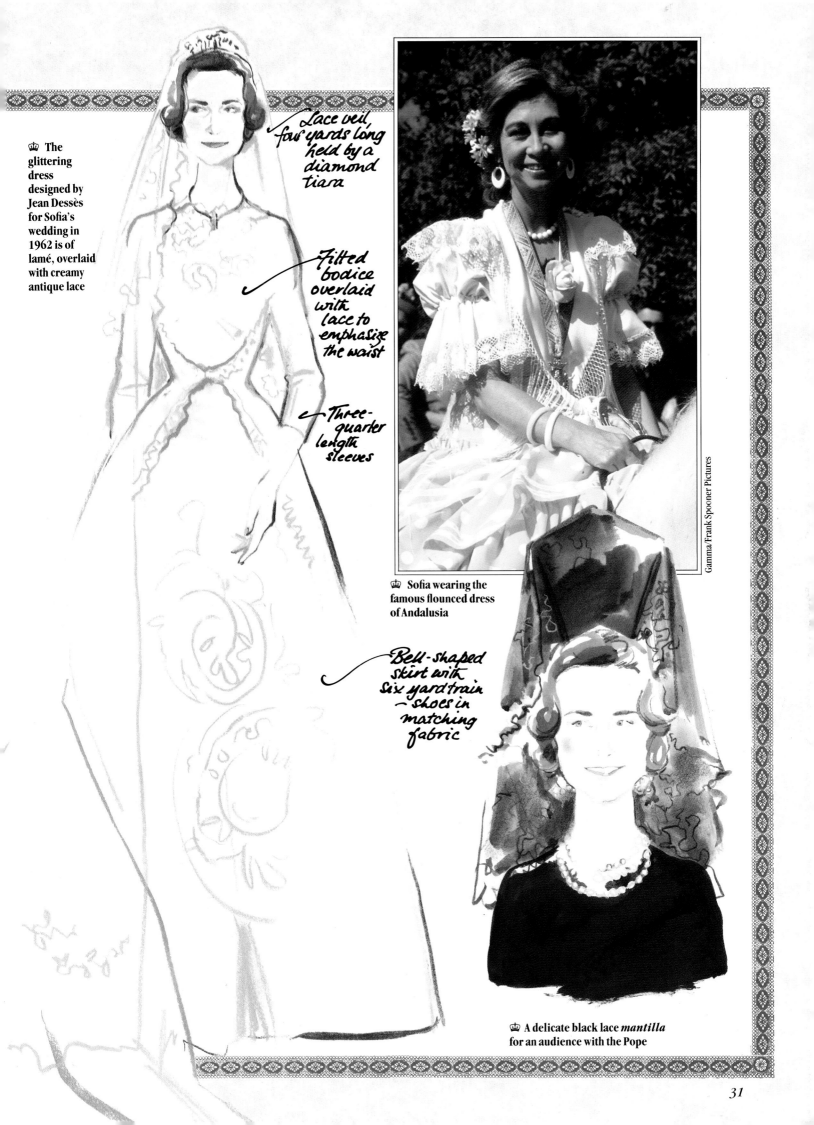

♛ The glittering dress designed by Jean Dessès for Sofia's wedding in 1962 is of lamé, overlaid with creamy antique lace

Lace veil, four yards long held by a diamond tiara

Fitted bodice overlaid with lace to emphasize the waist

Three-quarter length sleeves

Bell-shaped skirt with six yard train — shoes in matching fabric

Gamma/Frank Spooner Pictures

♛ Sofia wearing the famous flounced dress of Andalusia

♛ A delicate black lace *mantilla* for an audience with the Pope

31

♔ Sofia often goes hatless but, for formal occasions, prefers wide-brimmed styles like this cool summer straw

no hat or gloves

Alice band worn with bouffant hairstyle

♔ The 'eighties look, combining chic with practicality. A linen dress and jacket in an original colour scheme, combining sandy beige with navy blue

Gilt buttons on pockets and fastenings

minimal jewellery — just simple pearl necklace and bracelet

Full-flared skirt just below the knee

♔ A typical 'sixties style – a slim slip of a dress, with striped top and plain skirt, worn on an informal trip to Rome

Classic court shoes with high heels

👑 This sumptuous dinner gown has a distinctly Spanish air. It was worn for the couple's State visit to England

Black cloqué velvet with a deep scalloped neckline

Tightly-fitted red moiré cummerbund

Full skirt banded with blue satin ribbon

👑 For their State visit to England in 1986, Sofia wore a simple coat and sombrero hat. Juan Carlos is in full-dress uniform

Elegant accessorizing —Jewelled earrings and one perfectly placed brooch

👑 The wide-shouldered look, brilliantly carved in candy pink silk with black ribbon trim and a slender black skirt

33

Rex Features

THE YEARS OF WAITING

JUAN CARLOS AND SOFIA EMBARKED ON MARRIED LIFE LIKE ANY YOUNG COUPLE BUILDING A FAMILY. BUT WHEN GENERAL FRANCO ANNOUNCED THAT AFTER HIM, SPAIN WOULD HAVE A KING ONCE MORE, DESTINY BECKONED

BY MARCH 1964, JUAN CARLOS AND SOFIA had settled in at La Zarzuela with little Elena. Juan Carlos was heard to claim happily, 'Perhaps not all homes are palaces, and not every palace a home, but certainly a home is a home when there is a child present.'

From the very beginning, Sofia was determined to fulfil all her new roles as mother, wife and Princess: 'I believe that a wife's role should be to help her husband but without losing her independence. My aim is to make my husband happy, without failing to remain at the service of Spain.'

Sadly, Sofia was to suffer a tragedy in her own family when, on 6 March of that year, her father, King Paul of Greece, died at the age of 63. It was a hard blow for the Princess, and only the presence of her husband and her daughter by her side could tide her over. Sofia's brother became Constantine II. His life would now be full of responsibilities, and he was eager to share his future experiences as King of Greece with his sister and new brother-in-law, so a close friendship developed between the Greek and Spanish Royal Houses.

In September of that same year, Juan Carlos and Sofia went to Greece to attend a happier event – Constantine's marriage in the Cathedral at Athens to Princess Anne-Marie of Denmark. The new Royal couple had met and fallen in love at Juan Carlos and Sofia's wedding.

Another pregnancy

Juan Carlos was now 26 years old and much of his time was still spent in studying the detailed workings of the Spanish State and its government. He gathered information and gained practical experience of every Ministry, in anticipation of a future role which, in a Spain still gripped by Francoism, was as yet by no means certain. Much of Juan Carlos's research involved visits to different provinces, and he was always accompanied by Sofia. Already familiar with English,

she had mastered the Spanish language within two years.

But there was also time for some personal interests. His early naval training had left Juan Carlos with a fascination for all things technological. However, Sofia, with her own love of classical music, found it difficult to share his taste in popular music.

He established what became known as his

♛ A thoroughly modern couple, Juan Carlos and Sofia happily shared all aspects of early married life with gusto: Sofia frequently accompanying her husband on his favourite leisure activity – sailing; and the Royal couple delighting in the upbringing of their infant daughters, Elena and Cristina

'communications room' filled with up-to-date musical equipment and, later, a radio receiver. Conveniently, the room was right next to his study – an ideal place for him to take an occasional break from his work.

By the end of 1964, Sofia was delighted to find that she was pregnant again, and on 13 June 1965, Princess Cristina Federica Victoria arrived, born in the same room of the hospital as Princess Elena, and – later – Prince Felipe. As with Elena, Cristina's baptism was a great occasion, attended by various ranks of international nobility.

Juan Carlos and Sofia's pleasure at the new arrival was undisguised, and when the first misgivings about the lack of a male heir began to be voiced in the ever-vigilant press, the Prince was quick to dismiss them with the remark: 'I wouldn't change either of my daughters for the world!'

The quiet years

These were essentially the quiet years for Juan Carlos and Sofia. With their daughters, Elena and Cristina, they lived happily at Zarzuela, making occasional visits to Portugal, Greece and Switzerland. They also made occasional State visits, taking their daughters with them whenever possible.

On the whole, however, State visits were rare, not least because of the lack of a clear-cut constitutional role for Juan Carlos. In 1966, General Franco had introduced the 'Organic Law of the State', which confirmed the restoration of the monarchy in Spain in case of his death or incapacity. The implication was that the Generalissimo was 'grooming' Juan Carlos to take over from him, but nothing had been said officially.

The fact remained that although Juan Carlos and Sofia lived in splendid surroundings, and had enjoyed all the pageantry of a memorable Royal wedding, their position ultimately rested upon the decisions of an ageing military dictator. The future of monarchy throughout Europe was made all the more uncertain for the couple when, in 1967, Sofia's brother, King Constantine, having ruled over Greece for only three years, was removed by a military coup and forced into temporary exile in Paris before finally moving to London.

The dynasty assured

On 30 January 1968, Sofia gave birth to her third child. A nurse, seen hurriedly departing from the delivery room, whispered the news to the reporters impatiently awaiting Juan Carlos. *'Es precioso, rubio y con ojos azules'* – a beautiful, fair-haired and blue-eyed boy. At last, the long-awaited heir to the Bourbon dynasty had arrived. Juan Carlos could not restrain his

Topham

emotions, shouting, 'It's a boy' as he waved to the crowds outside the hospital: 'Spain has one more to serve her!'

The new arrival's full tally of Christian names was announced in an official bulletin from Juan Carlos which explained why he was given each one: 'He shall be named Felipe, in accordance with our dynastic traditions; Juan after my father and myself; Pablo [Paul] after his maternal grandfather, King of Greece; and Alfonso in memory of Alfonso XIII.'

A week after Felipe's birth, relatives began to arrive in Madrid for the christening at La Zarzuela. It was a Royal family reunion on a scale that had not been seen in Spain since before the Civil War nearly 40 years earlier. Queen Victoria Eugenie had not set foot in Madrid for 37 years. She had always said that she would return if a Bourbon heir was born, and now, as good as her word, she arrived for the christening of her great-grandson, greeted at Madrid Airport by some ten thousand of her erstwhile subjects and her own grandson, Juan Carlos.

In the presence of over two hundred members of family and selected guests, the Infante Felipe was baptized by the Archbishop of Madrid at La Zarzuela.

Among those present at the ceremony was General Franco. Queen Victoria Eugenie came forward to confront the *Caudillo* for the first time since 1921. 'Now you have three more Bourbons from which to choose,' she said, 'father, son and grandson.'

Within a year, the silver-haired Queen — considered, in her time, to be the most beautiful of all Spanish queens — would be dead. She was buried with due ceremony in Lausanne.

♛ *The birth of Felipe in 1965 completed the family and assured the Bourbon dynasty for another generation. Although aware of their Royal destiny, Juan Carlos and Sofia were determined to give their children a normal childhood*

Rex Features

Hulton-Deutsch Collection

AT HOME AT LA ZARZUELA

A modest two-storeyed building, the Zarzuela Palace echoes the informal life style of the Spanish Royals, with tennis and squash courts, a swimming pool and cosy but elegant interiors redesigned by Sofia

Robert Hunt Library

Rex Features

Agencia Efe

Camera Press

Europa Press

♛ *In 1969, Franco announced his successor: Juan Carlos – and not his father, Don Juan. On 23 July, in the Zarzuela Palace, Juan Carlos officially accepted his nomination* top. *Known as their Royal Highnesses from now on, Prince Juan Carlos and Princess Sofia had new official roles and duties to fulfil* inset above

THE BECKONING THRONE

In the middle of 1969, General Franco took a long-awaited decision that would change Juan Carlos and Sofia's lives for ever. Addressing the *Cortes* (Spanish Parliament) with great solemnity, he announced the future to his citizens: 'Conscious of my responsibility before God and History, and having weighed with due objectivity the qualities united in the person of Juan Carlos de Bourbon, I have decided to propose him to the nation as my successor.' A vote was taken, and by a considerable majority the Law of Designation was passed. From that moment on, Juan Carlos would carry the official title of Prince of Spain, and would receive all the rights decreed by that role. Spain could now look to its future.

With Juan Carlos's new role, protocol and State duties inevitably took over during the course of the coming years. The next five years, in particular, were to see a huge number of State visits around Europe and the rest of the world.

In June 1970, Prince Juan Carlos and Princess Sofia returned to London with their three children for the Queen Mother's birthday celebrations. From there, they visited France, where they were the official guests of President Pompidou and established the beginnings of a lifelong friendship with future President Giscard d'Estaing. In the United States, they were entertained at the home of Senator Edward Kennedy.

An ordinary Royal Family

Princess Sofia captured the hearts of the American people with her charm, elegance and unaffectedness. In an interview with the American press she remarked, 'I enjoy home life, being with my children and just taking things as they come. I lead a simple life; you might say that I'm just an ordinary person.'

This 'ordinariness' was to come out in the Royal couple's attitude to their family. Elena and Cristina had been educated in England with other children at St Mary's School, Ascot, and things were to be no different for the Bourbon heir, Felipe. He would go to the School of Los Rosales in Madrid. Juan Carlos himself declared: 'His education shall be open and free, as befits the nature of our times.'

They also went to Iran, Japan and, in 1973, to England for the wedding of Princess Anne and Captain Mark Phillips.

As often as they could, all three children

would accompany Prince Juan Carlos and Princess Sofia on their foreign visits. With increasing State pressures, private moments with the family would become all the more precious. Whenever possible, the family were together – either in Madrid or at their newly acquired family home, Marivent, in Majorca, where they were able to pursue their interests in outdoor sports in relative privacy. Always a keen sportsman, Prince Juan Carlos maintained his interest in sailing, and in 1972 took part in the Munich Olympics as part of the sailing team with his yacht *Fortuna*.

The couple also continued to explore their own country: provincial tours to Catalonia, Asturias and Andalusia followed one after another. They visited factories, mines and hospitals, where Princess Sofia's concern for those most in need – the young, the poor and the distressed – was always remarked upon and admired. 'There is no greater satisfaction to me,' she said, 'than that of entering the home of any family, in any country, and having them talk with me of their lives and their problems.'

The student Princess

In 1974, Princess Sofia enrolled in a humanities course at the University of Madrid. On Saturday mornings, she would arrive, dressed simply and elegantly, to sit down among her fellow students. She was steadily establishing herself as being first and foremost a Spaniard; when she was asked how it felt to be Greek by background and German by education, she immediately replied: '*muy española*' (very Spanish).

There were undoubtedly some difficult years for Prince Juan Carlos and Princess Sofia. The increasing political unrest in Spain – particularly in the Basque and Catalonian provinces, where rebellions against General Franco's repressive regime was strongest – did little to enhance Spain's reputation abroad. Matters were not helped by the assassination in 1973 of Spain's Prime Minister, Carrero Blanco, by the Basque extremist group ETA. During these years, it took all of Juan Carlos's considerable skills as a diplomat to maintain friendly relations with other countries.

He was greatly aided in this by Princess Sofia, ever by his side to offer encouragement and advice when it was needed. He was also finding it necessary to dedicate more time to affairs of State. The prospect of his apprenticeship coming to an end was getting ever closer as, in 1975, General Franco became increasingly ill and the Prince, for one, brief period after another, would take over the reins of government.

Meanwhile, in the Spanish Sahara, territorial disputes were becoming more and more serious, with the possibility of war growing ever nearer.

The Prince takes charge

With General Franco lying critically ill in hospital, Prince Juan Carlos was forced to make the first major State decision of his life. After first consulting his advisers, he then turned to Princess Sofia, whose reply was firm: 'I think a general's place is with his troops.' On Sofia's birthday, 2 November, the Prince flew out to the Sahara: 'At all costs the troops' morale was to be raised, but war must be avoided also.' He believed his duty as Honorary Captain-General of the Armed Forces was 'to be the first soldier of Spain', and he succeeded in the Spanish Sahara where perhaps all others would have failed.

Prince Juan Carlos returned to Madrid and three weeks later, after more than a month of growing steadily weaker and weaker, General Francisco Bahamonde Franco died on 20 November. Prince Juan Carlos's time had come. But would he ascend the throne as the puppet of Franco's supporters or as an independent monarch?

'*A general's place is with his troops*'

SOFIA TO JUAN CARLOS

Hulton-Deutsch Collection

👑 *Poised in the wings to take over from the old guard, Prince Juan Carlos played an increasingly prominent and responsible part in Spain's affairs of State above, as Franco's health deteriorated. The heavy burden of a monarchy renewed finally came to rest on his shoulders when the aged dictator died in November 1975 below*

Camera Press

A GALLERY OF LOVE

While maintaining the glamour and graciousness of the Spanish Royal tradition, King Juan Carlos and Queen Sofia have also set their indelible stamp on it with their informal and active life style which makes them readily accessible to people at home and abroad. Yet, what they prize above all else are their close family ties. Fond memories, for them, are chiefly associated with happy times spent together with their children, taking part in the activities they love best

♛ Informal portraits of the children *top right* were commissioned by Juan Carlos and hang in the Zarzuela Palace. Ricardo Macarrón, the King's favourite artist, also did the charming study of Sofia *right*

♛ The crib that awaited Elena. Juan Carlos and Sofia proudly displayed it to the nation along with other items of layette for their first-born

AISA

Hulton-Deutsch Collection

Elena

Cristina

Felipe

 Far from home, Sofía instinctively responds to a mother and child *right*

 Juan Carlos messes about on *Fortuna*, the yacht he entered for the Olympics *below right*

 The family relaxes at Marivent, their holiday home in Majorca *below*

Rafael Samano/Cover

Gonzales Llenas/Cover

Europa Press

Pepperfoto

On 22 November 1975 – in a brief 45-minute ceremony – Juan Carlos was proclaimed King of Spain in the Cortes (Spanish Parliament) – the first time a Spanish monarch had been admitted there for over 50 years. Above *At midday, Juan Carlos and Sofia entered the chamber.* Top right *The Cortes rose as Juan Carlos, with his right hand on the Bible, took his oath of office, the Spanish crown, sceptre and cross – secular symbols of the monarchy – resting on a gold-embroidered velvet pillow in the foreground.* Centre and opposite *The new King made his proclamation speech to the Cortes. Behind him were leading figures of the Church, State and army, Sofia and their three children. Other members of his family watched from the public galleries. The speech was interrupted several times by applause from the House*

A KING FOR ALL SPAIN

**IN NOVEMBER 1975, JUAN CARLOS WAS KING AT LAST.
AN ATTEMPTED COUP IN 1981 PROVIDED HIS SEVEREST
TEST BUT, WITH SOFIA AT HIS SIDE, HE TRANSFORMED
THEIR BELOVED SPAIN FROM DICTATORSHIP TO DEMOCRACY**

O N THE MORNING OF 22 November 1975, Prince Juan Carlos, accompanied by Sofia and their children, arrived at the Cortes to be invested as the first Bourbon King of Spain for nearly 45 years. Watching from the gallery of the building's main chamber were Royal relatives and guests, including the Duke of Edinburgh, Juan Carlos's sisters, Pilar and Margarita, and the exiled King Constantine of Greece and his wife Queen Anne-Marie.

Before Parliament and people, the Prince took his oath, with a message that was brief and direct: 'A free and modern nation needs the participation of all its citizens ... Justice is the prerequisite of liberty and the King is the first person who must fulfil his duty. I beg always the help of God in taking those most difficult decisions which we shall most certainly be required to confront, and I trust most fully in the virtues of the Spanish family. If together we remain united, the future shall be ours. VIVA ESPAÑA!'

Five days later, a mass honouring the occasion was celebrated at the church of Los Jeronimos, in Madrid. After the ceremony crowds cheered as their new King and Queen drove through the streets of Madrid in an open-topped car. At the Royal Palace, a gala reception was later held in their honour.

Mixed reaction

Spain's joy at her new King was not universal. In many places the immediate response to the Prince's Coronation was muted. The Spanish

♔ *Juan Carlos's proclamation as King marked a new era in Spanish history. However, the new monarchy was looked on with mistrust by many in Spain, who believed that Juan Carlos would simply be a puppet king who would continue Franco's policies. It would take all of his skills to prove them wrong*

people had spent much too long being held down by a single man and were suspicious that their new King would simply carry on the ways of the old General, or that he would be replaced by the military. 'It shall be the reign of Juan the Brief,' said one sceptical exiled politician. 'If the King wants a Crown,' ran a popular slogan, 'he can make it out of cardboard.' After years of standing two paces behind General Franco at ceremonies, Juan Carlos had come to be seen as ineffectual and weak.

But just as the General had misread his successor, so too the people of Spain were judging their new King unfairly. They failed to gauge both the sincerity of his intentions and his strength of personality. He and Sofia had seen enough to know that the only way forward for Spain was through change. Juan Carlos had expressed his wish to be 'A King for all Spain', a phrase that he interpreted to mean restoring those rights and liberties that every other country in Western Europe had been taking for granted for years. In June 1977, just 18 months after the Coronation, Spain enjoyed its first free general election since before the Civil War.

Family and State

In the meantime the new Royal Family intended to carry on much as usual. Within a week of the Coronation, Sofia was back at Madrid University continuing her humanities course. 'I thought I had to turn up as usual and break the ice, so that people could see nothing

Gamma/Frank Spooner Pictures

Rex Features

had changed,' she would later explain.

The family were not to change their residence; their home was to remain, as it had been for more than a dozen years, at La Zarzuela – the property of the Spanish National Trust. Although the enormous Palacio Real (Royal Palace), with its 3000 rooms, was theoretically at their disposal, it was clearly not suitable for a modern royal family with a strong preference for informality. It continued to be a venue for State occasions, but was never actually lived in by Juan Carlos and his family.

Not long after the Coronation the King and Queen began to make State visits around the world. While Spain under Franco had tended to be inward-looking, under the new guidance of Juan Carlos and Sofia this trend would be reversed. From now on, the new monarchs would take great trouble to open up wider horizons for their realm, travelling to many countries, including China, the Soviet Union, India and Japan. At the beginning of June 1976 they went to the United States together as the official guests of President Ford. Juan Carlos received a warm welcome in the White House, and also in Congress itself, where Senators and Congressmen alike gave the first monarch ever to address their ranks a huge standing ovation.

He also played up to the sport of press cross-examination. When asked how he and Sofia would spend the day if left to themselves he replied: 'Well . . . I suppose I'd end up doing what every other husband does. We'd go shopping and I'd have to carry all the bags back.'

On 14 May 1977, the King and Queen welcomed back Don Juan and Countess Maria at La Zarzuela. Don Juan was finally returning to his homeland, but first he had a formal duty to carry out. Before an assembled gathering he stepped forward and read a brief formal statement which ceded all his rights to the throne of Spain. It was a strange moment for the old man, to know that despite spending so long as first in line to the throne, he would never in fact rule Spain and that his own son had been chosen before him.

But at least he could now finally enjoy a future in Spain. These would be years of great political reconciliation. In 1980, King Alfonso's XIII's body was brought home to rest in the tombs of El Escorial.

Holidays in Majorca

By the mid-1970s, Juan Carlos, Sofia and the three children had established the custom of going to Majorca for their holidays. They had set up their 'summer Zarzuela' at the old, newly converted Greek museum of Marivent just out-

THE CORTES COUP

On Monday 23 February 1981, an extraordinary scene occurred at the Spanish *Cortes* that would provide a severe test to the new Spanish monarchy. At 6.25 pm, as the members of Parliament were swearing in their new president, Leopoldo Calvo-Sotelo, 200 armed members of the Civil Guard, led by Lt-Colonel Antonio Tejero *below,* stormed the building. The military rebels announced that they were taking over the Government and issued proclamations in Juan Carlos's name as if he had sanctioned the coup. As Spain waited anxiously, the King contacted each of the leading army generals, reiterating that he, and only he, was in charge of Spain's armed forces. At 1.30 am he appeared live on Spanish television and, in a moving but determined speech to the nation, denounced the rebels' coup. At 4.00 am, another leading rebel, General Millans del Bosch, withdrew his support of the coup, and by midday of 24 February Tejero had surrendered, the members of Parliament were released, and the coup had collapsed

Hulton-Deutsch Collection

Paco Junquera/Cover

♛ *With her warm personality, Sofia has become a natural ambassadress in her own right. Whether at public festivals* left, *or during private moments with her family at Marivent* above, *she is indispensable to Juan Carlos. His joy at greeting her in 1979 when she returned from India* below *was unconfined*

side the capital, Palma. Here they showed their appreciation of modern Spanish art by hanging the paintings of Salvador Dali and Miro, as well as more classic oil paintings by Goya and Delacroix. Above all, however, Marivent was a place of outdoor relaxation and activity, where Juan Carlos would continue his sailing and ride about on a motorbike, often with young Felipe on the back. As with so much else about the new Spanish Royal Family, the emphasis was on informality, and the suspicions of the Spanish people were gradually being thawed by the simplicity of their private lives and the relaxed, casual good humour of their public demeanour.

Juan Carlos himself was working extremely hard in his efforts to modernize Spain. He would be up at dawn each morning, and after an hour or two in his study would join the rest of his family for breakfast at 8.30. Still an enthusiastic sportsman, keen to keep himself fit, he would regularly play squash with the Wimbledon star, Manuel Santana. 'I have even managed to beat him once or twice,' said the King with pride.

The saviour of democracy

By February 1981, the brewing disappointment of General Franco's old supporters had turned into anger and a desire for action. Some weeks earlier, several junior officers had approached Juan Carlos to voice their dissatisfaction at the way things were going in Spain. Juan Carlos had been polite but firm: 'It is not the duty of an officer to interfere in affairs of State; the King and his subjects are a sovereign nation.' At the time he had thought no more about it, but his words were soon to prove significant.

On Monday 23 February, 200 armed members of the *Guardia Civil* (Civil Guard), led by Lt-Colonel Antonio Tejero, stormed the building of the Spanish *Cortes*, and announced that

45

they were taking over the Government. To Juan Carlos's dismay the military rebels began to issue proclamations in his name, as though he supported the attempted coup and had in some way encouraged it. Showing great determination, the king did two things which effectively suffocated the rebels' chances of success. Firstly he immediately contacted each of the nine leading army generals, reiterating that he was in charge of the Spanish Armed Forces and that they should take their orders from him. Secondly, he went on Spanish television live, condemning the events in the *Cortes* and demanding that Colonel Tejero give in.

The King's strong stance, combined with the complete lack of popular support for the rebels' actions, proved too much, and by the next day the coup folded. More importantly for Juan Carlos, however, it proved to the people of Spain that his support of democracy was sincere and that he would never again walk in the shadow of General Franco.

Into the 1980s

The year of 1981, which had begun so dramatically for Juan Carlos, ended on a note of personal sadness for Sofia when, in September, her mother, Queen Federika, died. She had come to Madrid for a minor eye operation but unexpected complications set in, and within a few days she was dead. The authorities in Greece consented to the funeral ceremony being held in Athens at Tatoi Palace with Constantine, Sofia and Princess Irene (now a renowned concert pianist) all in attendance, and the ex-King following the hearse on horseback.

It had been a watershed year. Spain was coming up to its third democratic elections in October of the next year, and Juan Carlos made it quite clear that whoever would be the next Prime Minister, whatever his political colouring, it was his duty as a democratic monarch to support him. It has been a mark of his success in upholding this neutrality that most Socialist Party members consider themselves 'juancarlists'.

The children

In the meantime, the education of Juan Carlos and Sofia's children was well under way. By 1983, Elena had left the English school of St Mary's, Ascot, to begin her university career at ESCUNI (a university school in Madrid), where she would study to become a teacher and become the first Spanish princess to have a university degree. Also in this year, Cristina came to England (where she stayed with Constantine and Anne-Marie, by now living in London) to do a language course, before going on to Madrid University. Felipe, meanwhile, embarked on a period of study at Lakefield College, Canada. In 1985, he would enter the Military Academy at

Alpha

👑 *By the time of Juan Carlos and Sofia's visit to Britain in 1986* above, *it was clear that the previous 'rift' over the Gibraltar issue had been well and truly forgotten. Today, relations between the two Royal Families are extremely close, and Prince Charles, in particular, has often expressed his admiration of the Spanish King. The warmth and depth of their affection can be seen in this relaxed and informal picture, taken during one of Charles and Diana's many regular visits to Marivent*

👑 Below *Juan Carlos and Sofia look relaxed and happy at a Literary Award ceremony outside the historic University of Alacala de Henares*

Tim Graham

Miguel Gonzalez/Cover

Saragossa like his father, Juan Carlos, had done before him.

The 1980s saw their inevitable quota of State visits, culminating in Juan Carlos and Sofia's 1986 trip to Britain – the first visit by a Spanish monarch since 1905, when Alfonso XIII had put in an appearance at Buckingham Palace.

Anglo-Spanish relations

In 1981, there had been a slight political rift between England and Spain, over the re-emergence of the 'Gibraltar issue', which led to Juan Carlos and Sofia's feeling unable to attend Charles and Diana's wedding that year. Now, as the Spanish Royal couple were greeted at Heathrow by the Prince and Princess of Wales, any rift there might have been was clearly over. On the evening of their arrival Juan Carlos and Sofia were honoured at a banquet at Windsor Castle, and on the next day, Juan Carlos became the only European monarch ever to address the assembled Houses of Parliament.

Later, the couple went up to Oxford, where Juan Carlos was awarded an honorary doctorate by the late Lord Stockton. It was a highly successful visit and, one year later, Charles and Diana themselves went to Spain. Relations between the two Royal Families were further cemented less than three months later, when Charles and Diana returned yet again to spend a brief holiday at the 'summer Zarzuela' in Marivent.

A BLOODLESS REVOLUTION

Under the forward-looking guidance of Juan Carlos and Sofia, Spain has emerged from the stagnation of Francoism to become a thriving Western democracy. Today, she is a member of the EEC and, for the first time in 50 years, enjoys many liberties, such as freedom of the press, that other democracies have always taken for granted. Above all, this dramatic revolution has been brought about without strife or political and economic chaos

Tim Graham

Image Bank

A PLACE IN THE SUN

♛ In 1987 the Spanish magazine Hola! produced a special issue to celebrate Juan Carlos and Sofia's silver wedding anniversary. In 25 years their marriage seems to have caught the spirit of what modern Spain seeks from its monarchy. Informal without being ordinary, impartial without being indifferent, and strong-willed without being dictatorial, they have helped to establish a new Bourbon dynasty that stands every chance of flourishing into the next century and beyond

In May 1987, Juan Carlos and Sofia celebrated their silver wedding anniversary. In the 25 years of their marriage, they have gone from strength to strength, gaining a new international respect for the Spanish monarchy and the love and support of their people.

With the Spanish monarchy's exile well and truly over, Juan Carlos can now keep in contact with all the members of his family with greater ease. His sisters, Margarita and Pilar, are happily married and living in Spain with families of their own, and his parents, Don Juan and Countess Maria, have settled in a quiet residential suburb of Madrid. Father and son enjoy a happy relationship.

Most of the year is still spent at Zarzuela. Sofia maintains her strong interests in charity and welfare, and also has a great interest in the cultural renaissance that has taken place in Spain since Franco's death. She steers away from any political involvement, but it is clear that her advice as a wife is both shrewd and sensible. Undeniably a modern queen, her contemporary interests and concerns have been invaluable to the new role of the Spanish monarchy.

For Juan Carlos himself, between the long hours of State business to which he still commits himself, there must be time for a profound satisfaction at the way things have worked out. Born an exile and brought up as trainee accomplice to a military dictator, he cannot have dared to hope for the way of life that his country and his family now enjoy. While Spain has attained ever higher levels of freedom and stability, the monarchy has been accepted in a way that very few would have expected. There are a son and heir to the throne, two bright and pretty daughters and, above all, a wife who has done so much to help and support her husband. 'I listen to lots of people,' says the King, 'and receive advice from all quarters, which I then think over. But the truth is that I don't marry myself to anyone's forces. Marry? I am only married to Sofia.'

> ### 'Marry? I am only married to Sofia'
> #### JUAN CARLOS